AND IT CAME TO PASS

IN THE NEW TESTAMENT

By Eric Scott

36 BIBLE STORIES FOR GROWN-UPS

And It Came To Pass
In The New Testament:
36 Bible Stories for Grown-Ups

Copyright © 2017 by Eric Scott

All rights reserved. No part of this book may be reproduced
or transmitted in any form or by any means
without written permission of the author.

ISBN-13: 978-0-9981829-6-4

Printed in the United States of America

RevMedia Publishing

PO BOX 5172, Kingwood, TX 77325

No part of this book may be reproduced or transmitted in any
form or by any means, electronic or mechanical—including
photocopying, recording, or by any information storage and
retrieval system—without permission in writing from the publisher.

Unless otherwise noted, all Scripture references are taken from
the King James Version. Used by permission.

Forward

For years I have enjoyed studying and teaching the Bible, as a lay person, a professional theologian, and now as a lay person again. After obtaining degrees in biology and business administration at major universities I launched a career in swimming pool water purification. My work at two Fortune 100 corporations led me to become CEO of a small chemical manufacturing company. Having been deeply involved in local churches most of my life I sensed a spiritual calling and enrolled in one of America's most renowned seminaries as a middle-aged businessman with a family of four.

I have pastored churches, visited excavated sites in the Holy Land, led seminars, preached in stadiums, and attended hundreds of church related events rubbing elbows with people of virtually every Christian denomination. After years of studying and lecturing I no longer count myself an expert on the Bible. I am now simply another humbled seeker. I remain on a spiritual quest though I am no longer a religious institutionalist. Some who read this will relate.

My wife and I invested our retirement funds in a small restaurant where I never tire of mixing with smart people who may, or may not, share my Christian perspective. I particularly like to spar with intelligent, well-educated people of diverse backgrounds over contentious religious matters and controversial current events. I have discovered that decent people can enjoy sincere well-founded dialog and grow from each other's genuine peculiar beliefs. Iron sharpens iron according to an insightful proverb.

I am greatly encouraged by how interested people I engage with are about spiritual issues. However, I'm amazed at how ignorant most folks are about the Bible, itself. I find it amusing, though somewhat annoying, how dogmatic some individuals can be about their particular religious views, and how quickly they become put off by someone else's genuinely held beliefs, or lack thereof. Dogmatism and naivety both kill dialog, and one of my greatest concerns is for people who have developed a jaundiced view of the Bible, organized religion, or even God, based on what they've observed in others who say they're Christian.

Sadly today, capable persuasive secular antagonists twist science and alter history in a relentless quest to discredit the Bible. I still think of science as an objective pursuit of reality, though much of what's parleyed as science today is actually little more than the promotion of unresolved agendas from various vested positions. On issues ranging from world climate to a healthy personal diet, too many of us are painstakingly diligent about spreading our biased misinformation. The same holds true in religious thought. There is a difference between constructive debate and self-serving manipulation.

<u>And It Came To Pass</u> is a simple overview of the Bible based on my understanding with a lot of input from various sources over many years of study. I happen to believe the stories in this book, but they are filtered through my own experience and analysis. Hopefully, my unconventional rendering of these familiar stories will provide fresh insight for your next religious conversation. This project is not authorized by any party or group. My conclusions are not documented or sourced. The stories are abbreviated and abridged for the sake of expedience and concision. Scripture quotations are from the Authorized King James translation of the Holy Bible or my own rendering of it. I hope this book makes you reflect on what

you believe and why you believe a particular way.

The Holy Bible is a single story composed of 66 books. The Old Testament consist of 39 books and covers the period from man's beginnings, or genesis, to the period around 400 BC when sacred Jewish history went silent. The 27 books in the New Testament address the life of Jesus of Nazareth and the establishment of the Christian Church. I have broken this project into two parts to make it more manageable for readers, but the two are inseparably linked. It doesn't matter where you start or what stories you are attracted to, but realize that all the stories together make a single story that is the essence of the Holy Bible. I included a couple of inter-testament period stories in the latter book to synthesize the two and fill in some needed information. May this effort bless your life, as my quest to understand and explain the Holy Bible blesses mine.

Table of Contents

Part 1: New Will & Testament

Chapter 1: The Greek Conquest 15

Chapter 2: Spread of the Roman Empire 19

Chapter 3: Taxing Circumstances 23

Chapter 4: Rebuilding the Temple 27

Chapter 5: Antagonistic Alliances 31

Chapter 6: A Plan Comes Together 35

Chapter 7: Mary and Joseph 41

Chapter 8: Jesus' Birth and Infancy 45

Chapter 9: Curious Star 49

Chapter 10: Jesus' Childhood 55

Part 2: Jesus' Ministry

Chapter 11: Reunion at the River 61

Chapter 12: A Wedding at Cana 65

Chapter 13: Cleansing Begins at the Temple 69

Chapter 14: Night Visitor 73

Chapter 15: Twelve Disciples 77

Chapter 16: Conversation at a Well 81

Chapter 17: Ministry of Healing 85

Chapter 18: What Jesus Taught 89

Chapter 19: Miracles, Signs, and Wonders 93

Chapter 20: Aggravating Religious Leaders 97

Chapter 21: Raising Lazarus 101

Part 3: The Christ's Mission

Chapter 22: Confronting the Establishment 107

Chapter 23: A Last Supper Together 111

Chapter 24: Arrest in a Garden 117

Chapter 25: Mock Trial 121

Chapter 26: A Hill Called Calvary 127

Chapter 27: Living Man in a Dead Body 131

Chapter 28: Impact on Observers 135

Part 4: The Church Era

Chapter 29: The Gift of Native Tongues 143

Chapter 30: The Early Christian Church 147

Chapter 31: Paul, Apostle to the Gentiles 151

Chapter 32: The Church's Mission 155

Chapter 33: End of Earth 159

Chapter 34: Rapture, Tribulation and Judgment 163

Chapter 35: Ultimate Humanity 169

Chapter 36: New Testament Overview 173

Prelude

It seems the Holy Bible isn't revered as it once was. Efforts to have it shunned or even legally banned from the public arena have been largely successful. Many young people today have had little or no exposure to it. You can attend a variety of churches and never come to really know their foundational document. Those who are familiar with fundamental Scriptures too seldom engage in pursuits that expand their comprehension or engrain biblical precepts into their constitution.

Even children can gain from exposure to the Bible's moral tenets, but it's not a quick easy read. Because it contains colorful characters and dynamic events that relate to our history and Earth's geography, watered down accounts provide fun reading matter for kids at bedtime. <u>And It Came To Pass In the New Testament</u> is a resource for serious adults who have a good idea what the Bible is about, but may question its validity, premise, significance, relevance or importance. If the Bible is what it clearly purports to be, it should be taken very seriously.

Much of what's contained in these Bible-based stories won't jive with some common notions. You won't see a beam of light from a star shining down on a baby in a feed trough like a giant spotlight. John the Baptist is not depicted as an unkempt half-baked fanatic screaming at passersby in the desert. And Jesus doesn't simply stroll along a fishing dock and casually ask a few random strangers to walk off their jobs and wander a few thousand miles with him while he teaches them complexities of Torah.

You will envision Bible characters as real people and epoch stories as legitimate events. You'll come to appreciate that each person and every event is recorded for a purpose. There were miracles to be sure, though you may not know how to fully assimilate them. You will learn to bite off what you can chew, chew what you can swallow, and swallow what you can digest. As Jesus used to teach, you become the words and thoughts you consume.

If you read this book all the way through and follow it up with research at a library or on the internet, you will see that the Bible is a lot more relevant and believable than you might have previously thought. In fact, you'll find that the Bible is intellectually dependable and offers feasible answers to questions that really matter. When you learn to decipher the mysteries that are shrouded in plain sight, you'll begin to connect dots that bring order and purpose to your life and man's existence on Earth.

Aside from gaining a better scientific and historical perspective, you'll also begin to realize why Jews, and Christians by extension, believe their God is unique; how there can be so many religious denominations that share a common denominator of core belief; and why sincere Christians can't compromise on controversial social matters they deem crucial to their faith. The aim is to open closed minds to explore viable probabilities.

Some people dogmatically insist the words in their particular translation of the Bible are to be interpreted verbatim. Unfortunately, most folks who hold that view don't benefit from a working knowledge of the original languages and cultures from which the text was derived. Some hold the view that the Bible is a collection of useful illustrations and allegories that various ancient writers were mysteriously inspired to record for mankind's eventual discovery. They rationalize and intellectualize the sacred text into total impotence. If you dissect a living body you gain insights about its structure, but you forfeit what gave it life.

Of course, there are those who dismiss the Bible as a bundle of fantastic myths and fables written by ambitious imposters and gathered by manipulative clerics to impose their worldview on ignorant underlings. The Bible recognizes all points of view, declaring, "Every man is right in his own eyes." The premise of the Bible is that it doesn't matter what you think. Truth is truth whether we recognize it, understand it, and accept it, or not. The Bible accommodates every opinion proposing that, "Now we see the world through murky glass. Only when we shed our physical trappings will we see things as they really are."

The Bible is so intricate and complex it couldn't be fully mastered by the most intelligent scholar in an extended lifetime of study. Yet, it's so simple that children are able to comprehend its essential tenets. The Bible is "milk for babes in faith, and meat for those who have grown to digest it." This book extrapolates essential elements into short stories about selected people, topics, and events that are widely known, sometimes disputed, and often misunderstood. When you question something, just keep reading. The stories come together and make sense when they converge in the end.

Every chapter of this book is designed to be an independent story, so you can pick and choose what you would like to read by topic according to your interests. However, it is designed to unfold chronologically and help establish a rational perspective from a 21st century biblical worldview. The whole is greater than the sum of its parts. Try not to get bogged down or diverted by questionable details until you see and can follow the master plan. Please allow me to open a window and shed new light from a different angle that might help you see more clearly some important biblical nuances you may have overlooked.

Part 1

New Will & Testament

1

The Greek Conquest

Territorial borders were not always clearly defined in the ancient world. Tribes, clans, and city-states claimed jurisdiction over what they could provide for and defend. Then, as now, only three sources of power dictated secular authority. Brute strength, sphere of influence, and reputation determined who dominated and who paid homage.

In the sixth century BC small unaffiliated groups, like the nomadic clans that dotted the Middle Eastern landscape, exerted brute strength and were only kept at bay by coalitions that formed unions through treaties. Those who feared they might face retribution from a recognized power didn't provoke weaker nations. That truth will determine the state of nations as long as men occupy a material Earth. An ambitious aggressive new force that aspires to gain independence or domination will always eventually arise among settled civilized nations.

The Persian Empire was splendid and vast. Under Persian rule, conquered states kept their cultural identity. Those who lived in the shadow of Persian domination enjoyed peace and safety because weaker leaders respected military strength. Wherever Persia's strength was questioned, it was tested. Rebellion has always percolated throughout the Middle East region. The absence or withdrawal of a Persian military presence invariably led to an outbreak of conflict in a given area.

Cyrus and Cambyses extended the rule of Persia west to the Aegean Sea, conquering small city states along the Greek coast. In 522 BC Darius came to power and set out to consolidate and strengthen the empire. From 500 to 494 BC he engaged the Greeks of Athens to put down a revolt. In 490 BC the Persians sent 25,000 trained and well equipped troops to advance on Europe. An army of 10,000 Athenians and Spartans surprisingly repelled them. The Persians went home. Ten years later Darius' successor, Xerxes, returned with what Greek historians referred to as a million man army. The Greek navy had a fleet of 350 ships and they were awestruck to see over a thousand vessels approaching.

The Greeks providentially retreated to the safety of their harbors while hundreds of Persian ships, including their armor and supply ships, were lost to a terrible storm in the bay overnight. The Greeks abandoned Athens and acquiesced to the advancing Persians who promptly burned their city. As they proceeded, the Persians realized the size of their army was unmanageable. Progress was slow, resources were scant, and the campaign was abandoned. Xerxes returned to Persia but left a small Army that skirmished with the Greeks for several decades. Over the course of those years the Greeks learned how to fight Persians, and win.

Around 430 BC Socrates gained notoriety as a great teacher in Athens. One of his students was a brilliant young man named Plato. In 387 BC Plato established the Athens Academy where the brightest, most promising young men of that age came to study science, art, literature, drama and philosophy. Plato became a man of great renown and taught a young prodigy by the name of Aristotle who arguably exerted more influence on the development of Western art, science, culture, philosophy and even military strategy than any man before or since. Aristotle's impact was greatly enhanced when he was given a sizable estate by King Philip II of Macedonia to personally tutor his son, Alexander, from the time he was thirteen until he was sixteen years old. Their correspondence indicates that a once excellent relationship soured in later years.

At the age of ten, Alexander was given a horse that could not be mounted. He broke the horse and rode it in every battle he engaged in over the next twenty years, and his battles were many. He was given charge of a command at the age of sixteen. His father once told him, "My boy, you must find a kingdom more suitable to your ambitions. Macedonia is too small for you." A military genius, Alexander the Great conquered and consolidated Greece, Sparta, Thrace, Illyria, and kept expanding.

He ran the Persians out of Europe and chased them back to their capital, capturing and claiming their territory. He extended his campaign into India, and died of malaria at the young age of thirty-three. His desire was to merge Greek and Oriental cultures, but instead the Hellenist culture dominated. In Alexander's wake the world learned to speak Greek, write in Greek, dress like Greeks, and even immolate Greek architecture.

Upon Alexander's demise, Greek territory was parceled out to his generals. Judah lay along the trade routes that connected Greece, Egypt, and the eastern reaches of Babylonia and India. The Hebrew tribes of the southern kingdom came home and resettled Yehuda. From now on the land of Israel would be referred to by its Greek equivalent, Judea.

As farmers, fishermen, tradesmen, and merchants prospered, they adopted Greek customs and ways. Secular society infiltrated the Temple. Rigid Hebrews strained to maintain their identity and values. Orthodoxy battled modernization and tradition yielded. Even common names changed. In simple terms, skipping the transitions, Simeon became Simon, Yochanon became John, Melchi became Malachi, and little boys named Yeshua, or Joshua, were called by their Greek equivalent, Iesous, that we know in English as Jesus.

2

Spread of the Roman Empire

When Alexander died, expansion ceased. His territory was parceled into five states and Judea eventually fell under the control of Seleucid Greek rulers. The Seleucids restricted Torah study and desecrated the Temple in an attempt to eradicate Jewish religion and culture. The Greeks sought to enlighten and modernize the Jews. They persecuted Jews who dared to cling to their religious beliefs and practiced their old ways.

In 166 BC the priestly Maccabee family rebelled and the Seleucids were forced to return autonomy to Israel. Like every dominant government that survived to maturity, Greece imploded. Leaders of Greek government, trade, military and the arts grew evermore socially sensitive and soft on enforcing time-honored standards. Diversity of expression led to cultural division. Lifestyle accommodations and political correctness set in. An advanced nation decayed. A vibrant aggressor crouched in waiting.

Rome was established in 753 BC. It was considered a Greek city in the fourth century BC. In 345 BC they began marching and by 290

BC Rome controlled half of the European continent. In the second century BC they conquered Carthage and by 146 BC mainland Greece was a Roman province. Pompey conquered Syria in 64 BC and the next year Aemilius Scauraus, Pomey's ambassador, went to Jerusalem.

The death of Hasmonean queen Alexandra Salome of Maccabean extraction plunged Judea into a civil war. Aristobulus ousted his older brother Hyrcanus as high priest. Hyrcanus appealed to King Arestas III of Nabataea who provided 50,000 soldiers and their joint forces set out to retake Jerusalem. Scaurus, the Roman General, met with both parties but accepted a bribe from Aristobulus to convince Arestas to lift his siege. As Arestas withdrew, Aristobulus, short on virtue, pursued and ambushed Arestas' unsuspecting army at Papyron.

Emperor Pompey arrived at Damascus in 63 BC and seeing the sibling rift as an opportunity, determined to pursue Judea himself. Josephus, the ancient historian, wrote, "When Pompey arrived at Jerusalem he surveyed the city and saw the walls were so firm it would be hard to overcome them; and the valley before the walls was terrible; and the temple that was in that valley was itself encompassed with a very strong wall, so that if the city were taken, the temple would be a second place of refuge for the enemy."

Aristobulus' soldiers resisted, but Hyrcanus' supporters opened a gate to let the Romans in, sparing blood but yielding to Rome. Pompey charged into the Temple to inspect it and desecrated the altar by entering the Holy of Holies, which only the High Priest should do. He divided the nation into Judea, Samaria, Galilee, Idumea and the coastal plain of Palestine. He placed the territory under Syrian taxing jurisdiction and returned to Rome with Aristobulus in chains. Hyrcanus was reinstated as High Priest to appease the people, but real power was vested in Antipater the Idumaean. Antipater was an Edomite descendant of Esau who converted to Judaism for political purposes. Rome was able to buy his loyalty.

In 49 BC Julius Caesar conquered what is now France and marched on Rome. He vanquished his opponents and ruled Rome for four years. Antipater prompted Hyrcanus to side with Caesar, so upon his victory the new emperor bestowed the title of Ethnarch on Hyrcanus and Procurator on Antipater. Antipater appointed his sons Phasael and Herod as military governors of Jerusalem and Galilee.

After Caesar's assassination in 44 BC, his lieutenant, Marcus Antonius, and nephew, Octavian, later known as Caesar Augustus, struggled for power. Hyrcanus and Antipater were under Marc Anthony's jurisdiction as ruler of Eastern Rome. Augustus became sole ruler and Marc Anthony would eventually die in the arms of Queen Cleopatra in Egypt.

Aristobulus' son, Antigonus Matthias, hired the Parthian army in 40 BC, invaded Syria, took Judea, decapitated Hyrcanus, killed Phasael, and claimed the Judean throne. Herod's family was besieged at Masada but Herod escaped to Petra then made his way to Rome. Supported by Marc Anthony, Herod was proclaimed "King of the Jews" by the Roman Senate and returned to Judea to claim his throne.

Herod began his campaign against Antigonus with the conquest of Galilee. He marched down the coast to take Jaffa and retook Masada, where his family was still hemmed in. He attacked Jerusalem hoping to bring a quick end to the war, but corrupt officers, mutinous troops, and Antigonus' guerrillas compelled him to abandon the siege. Reinforced by 6,000 of Marc Anthony's Roman soldiers, Herod approached Jerusalem again in 38 BC, but the onset of winter brought military operations to a halt. Spring ushered in a sabbatical year so instead of working the fields Jews came to Jerusalem to fight and put up a defense.

It took forty days for Herod's forces to breach the walled city, but the Jews still held the fortified Temple grounds. They asked Herod to permit the passage of animals and other offerings so sacrifices could continue. During the siege Antigonus used Herod's lack of pedigree as motivating propaganda, calling him a common Idumaean that wasn't even a real Jew, and questioning his right to the throne. Fearful for his legitimacy and acceptance, Herod complied with the request. Herod's forces eventually stormed in and despite his pleas for restraint, the brutal Roman troops acted without mercy, pillaging and killing everyone in their path, prompting Herod to complain to Marc Anthony.

Antigonus surrendered and was sent to Anthony to be featured in a military parade. Fearing Antigonus might win backing in Rome, Herod bribed Anthony to execute him. The Hasmonean's beheading in Antioch marked the first time the Romans executed a subjugated king. Herod also had 45 leaders of Antigonus' party put to death. Roman military custom dictated that captured kings were never executed out of deference and respect. That custom would surface again at Jesus' trial half a century later.

Herod's conquest of the kingdom was complete, and he began systematically exterminating the Hasmonean line that posed a potential threat to his reign. He ruled until his death in 4 BC. History records that Herod the Great was utterly ruthless, but could be charming when it was expedient. He killed and replaced wives when they offended him or he tired of them. He killed his own sons who came of age in order to preserve his throne. There was nothing he wouldn't do to secure the title that Rome bestowed on him, "King of the Jews".

3

Taxing Circumstances

King Herod the Great built grand palaces at the capital of Jerusalem, at his mountain retreat at Masada, and at Caesarea on the Mediterranean Sea coast. His opulent compounds boasted theatres and arenas that were open to the public. An Idumean who converted to Judaism, Herod didn't consider religion a spiritual enterprise, but a practical endeavor. He viewed himself as more Roman than Jewish, though his official title was "King of the Jews".

Roman engineers were assigned to build aqueducts to carry water from snowcapped mountains to cities and seaports miles away using cheap Jewish labor. The aqueducts also served as elevated highways that accommodated horses and chariots. Roads made of smaller stone blocks called pavers branched out to connect cities and served as trade routes. Roman soldiers went where they were needed quickly and efficiently. Roman aqueducts and roads were so well built that portions are still usable today.

To finance these elaborate construction projects Herod imposed heavy taxes on farmers, merchants and fishermen. Instead of sending outsiders to collect taxes, the Romans contracted local Jews who knew their culture, knew what their neighbors had, and how they got it. Publicans, as tax collectors were called, were despised as traitors, but attacking one was an assault on an agent of Rome.

To gain favor with the Jewish establishment and win over the common masses in 20 BC Herod determined to renovate the dilapidated Temple that was the epicenter of Jewish religion and culture. He spared no expense and completed the project in eighteen months. Thereafter he embarked on an elaborate building project continually expanding and improving the Temple grounds and related structures that lasted eighty years, long after his death.

Graft, corruption, and bureaucratic waste were commonplace in the government and in the Temple. Herod oversaw the affairs of state and reported to Rome. The Sanhedrin, a body of 70 elite clerics chaired by a Head Priest, administered day to day public affairs and worship activities. Roman soldiers were the federal patrol. Temple guards policed Jerusalem.

Jewish clerics were tasked with administering the Torah Mitzvot over Israel, much like Muslim clerics today impose the Koran's Sharia Law in Shiite states. Almost every civilized nation's code of conduct has been based on the religious temperament of its founder or ascendant leaders. That's still true of ancient jungle tribes, dessert clans, and modern superpowers alike. National life under Muslim clerics in Iran is quite different from government under Buddhist monks in Tibet, self-proclaimed gods in North Korea, avowed atheist presidents in Russia, or Christian presidents in the United States. Values dictate culture

Devout or secular, laws and the public behavior they guide and govern are adjusted over time by the beliefs, whims and desires of those who rise to power and exercise dominion. Willful leaders with strategically placed supporters can fundamentally change any enterprise to fit their belief system. Some Jews at the turn of the first century advocated that efficient government should be based solely on established principles. Others contended the government should allow for subjective interpretation. Then, as now, a block in power wanted to "conserve" traditional values. Some were willing to "moderate" the status quo. Those who didn't value tradition were more "liberal". And a "progressive" block sought to dismantle the old ways entirely and move on.

The prophet Samuel warned against institutional government. The Bible clearly states that every individual is accountable to God beyond his national or political affiliation or circumstance. The God of the Bible is consistently cast as a personal deity who utilizes institutions to test and mold the minds and hearts of men. People were formed to steward the Earth and be individually accountable for their conduct and contribution in the garden of life. That has not changed from the beginning.

Moses was handed ten commandments that were the basis for Torah Law. Priests from Aaron to Zechariah added hundreds of clarifications, addendums, and regulations. For example, the fourth command dictated that people, "Remember the Sabbath and keep it holy." The clarification was "relax, meditate on God, and don't exert yourself on Saturdays." Amplified regulations demanded that no cleaning, cooking, washing, mending, etc. were allowed on a Saturday under any circumstances. Priests even debated and regulated how many steps a person could take before he crossed the threshold of "exertion". It got ridiculous.

One of the most important elements the court regulated was the tithe. Purse strings are the reins of public direction. Abraham, father of the Jewish nation, offered Melchizedek one tenth of the spoil of an unprecedented military victory. The Jews adopted the practice of bringing a tenth of their personal gross revenue for Temple sacrifices and upkeep. By Herod's time the Jews administered a Temple tax, a civil tax, an infrastructure tax, and a benevolence tax.

Each year ten percent of every citizen's income went toward religious activities and feeding the priests. Ten percent went toward municipal operations in Jerusalem and feeding the priests. Ten percent went toward roads, bridges, and wall building, and feeding the priests. And every third year ten percent was given to care for widows and orphans, poor unemployable blind and crippled folks, and feeding the priests. The tax rate for Jewish citizens was effectively 33.33 percent. And priests were getting fat.

Rome exercised national jurisdiction and assessed separate taxes that were also onerous. A typical Roman tax rate for a successful Jewish merchant at the turn of the millineum ranged from ten to fifty percent, depending on the nature of his income and how well a publican liked him. A lot of coins never reached the Roman treasury. Not surprisingly, the people felt oppressed, but Caesar sensed he wasn't getting his fair share. And it came to pass while Herod the Great governed Judea that Caesar Augustus sent out a decree that every Roman province should gather a census and revise its tax rolls. Every Jew returned to his clan's town of origin. For example, those in King David's lineage traveled to David's great grandfather Boaz's barley farm and sheep ranch in Bethlehem to register.

4

Rebuilding the Temple

Before there were computerized data bases that tracked ancestries, Levite scribes recorded the birth of every child born into the Jewish race on scrolls. It was incumbent upon parents to make sure they registered the birth. Before there were policy manuals and codes of law, Hebrew clerical scribes acted as legal custodians. There were scribes whose great-great grandfathers guarded the same scrolls they were employed to maintain. There were even scribes assigned to oversee and check back-up copies. The Temple employed hundreds upon hundreds of record keepers, librarians, and administrators.

Today family trees make for a fascinating recreational hobby. Then, genealogy determined citizenship and established property rights and inheritances. We now have legal assistants and court reporters. The Sanhedrin had expert scribes at their disposal. If a specialist didn't have a ready answer, a scribal runner was sent to look up supporting facts and data and report back. No one could be a Levite scribe who didn't come from the clan of Levi and whose ancestry didn't indicate he was properly suited for the job.

Before Zechariah anointed Jeshua as Head Priest subsequent to the nation's return from Babylonia, he validated Jeshua's birth records to confirm a proper ancestral link to King David's chief priest. Every Saduccee could prove his bond to Zadok. Likewise, if anyone dared to reclaim King David's throne he would have to confirm his legal relationship to one of David's sons. Many clerics proposed the bloodline should run through Solomon since he followed David as king. Others believed Solomon's succession was broken by the prophet's curse on the house of Yeconiah, also known as King Jehoiachin, recorded in Jeremiah 22:30. Some scholars in Israel felt that a descendant of Nathan would be better suited to occupy the throne. That's why there are competing genealogies in the New Testament. Such a matter, if it arose, would have to be settled in the Sanhedrin.

Conflicts could usually be handled at the lowest level when laws or rights were questioned. If early Jews couldn't agree, they first took their issue before family or called in trusted friends. Local jurisdictions had elders whose counsel was generally accepted and followed. Only grave matters or issues of the highest urgency or importance were allowed to clutter the courts. The highest court was the Sanhedrin whose verdict was absolute. There was no further appeal. Any member of the Sanhedrin could judge a small matter. To make a civil judgment binding, a case had to be heard by at least three clerics and two of them had to agree. To judge a criminal case, only a couple dozen priests usually assembled because they needed twelve votes to seal a verdict by a majority of at least two.

When Jacob moved to Egypt the family was small and everybody knew each other's business. On his deathbed Jacob assigned Levi's descendants to be judges embedded among the other clans. When Moses brought the masses out of Egypt they had wagon loads of papyrus parchments and leather scrolls. Over the course of years, responsible Levites protected their sacred ancient records and kept them current. Families whose records were misplaced or ruined were outcast, as was the case after the Babylonian captivity. At no point had Jewish records been more combed and catalogued than when Herod funded the modern Temple compound in Jerusalem at the turn of the first century.

The priesthood was compromised by periodic strife, national displacement, and political intrusion, but all the records were brought up to date and such breaches and alterations were noted with asterisks and suitable footnotes. An industrious citizen might be able to prove his right to an inscripted gold chain he stumbled upon that had been given by a great ancestor to a distant relative or friend for safekeeping generations ago. If such a claim made its way to the Sanhedrin it would take three priests to hear the case and their majority determination after getting scribes to examine the records would be binding and irreversible. Needless to say, those who were more prominent in Israel shopped carefully for their prospective judges and offered to feed them. Common folks were being abused and becoming frustrated while corrupt priests continued getting fatter.

The Romans knew the Jews were evading taxes and offered bribes to Levite scribes who spied on Temple proceedings. Around 15 AD one of them got caught red-handed. The Head Priest, charged the spy with treason, a capital offense, and impulsively assembled at least twelve priests he knew he could influence. They returned a guilty verdict and the convict was immediately stoned to death outside the Temple grounds.

The Romans, who heretofore tried only infractions against Roman rule, were outraged and embarrassed. The matter came before Caesar Tiberius in Rome who deemed the Sanhedrin could continue to administer local justice in civil cases, but could no longer render a death penalty unless the acting local Roman Procurator confirmed and executed it. Convicted capital offenders could no longer be stoned to death by Jews. They would henceforth be crucified by Romans.

5

Antagonistic Alliances

Much of what we know about Jerusalem and the Jews who occupied it at the turn of the first century has come from extra-biblical contemporary historians like Josephus, Tacitus, and Philo. We've gained a wealth of information from literature discovered in Syria, Rome, Jordan and Egypt that described the nation and the race. Archeological digs have uncovered artifacts and implements that indicate cultural norms. Over a million Jews occupied Judea. Several hundred thousand lived in and around Jerusalem. Most of them were not particularly interested in politics or religion. But those who were seem to have defined and driven their culture. As with all nations through time, the general public was carried along.

Temple attendance was mandated, especially on prescribed holidays. Children were subjected to Torah training until they were at least eleven. Israel was always an inordinately literate and industrious society. Historians numbered those who were politically active as a small, almost miniscule, contingent. It's hard to differentiate religious activism from political activism because court was conducted in the

Temple and clerical priests administered the laws. Josephus estimated there were 10,000 Sadducees, 6,000 Pharisees, and 4,000 Essenes. At least 20,000 men were officially active in the Temple. We have no idea how many more sympathized with, supported, or identified with those major parties, but estimates range in the hundreds of thousands. There were also revolutionary insurrectionist groups like the Sicarii and the Zealots who attracted radicals but weren't counted because they weren't sanctioned and recognized by the establishment.

Sadducees were elite scholars who were generally secular and pragmatic. They tended to be legalistic and adhered strictly to Mosaic laws. They were notorious for finding creative ways to reinterpret established laws to their benefit. They were pious but didn't believe in spirits or life after death. They subscribed to morality based on a Torah code of ethics that they didn't seem particularly interested in applying within their own ranks. Sadducees operated under the creed of, "the end justifies the means."

Non-Levite Pharisees became recognized as clerics by virtue of their study and application of the Torah. They believed in angels and demonic spirits that interceded in the affairs of men on Earth. They viewed life as transitory and expected to live beyond the grave. Gnostics took their views even farther and proposed that anything physical was inherently evil, and everything spiritual was an actual piece of God.

Essenes were purists who ultimately turned their backs on Temple worship, believing evil men had corrupted God's intention. They lived in isolation and dedicated themselves to prayer, fasting, and Torah study. The Essenes likely were an offshoot of the Zadokites, or Sadducees, thus Levites. The Essene colony at Qumran passed down the famous Dead Sea scrolls. Scrolls that were stored in caves in the late first and early second centuries were rediscovered by a Beduoin shepherd in 1946. The once hotly contested scrolls have confirmed the literary accuracy of the modern Torah and the Christian Bible.

Religious Zealots openly opposed those who oppressed the masses and perverted their doctrines. Over the span of several decades they attacked the Romans and took back several outlying villages in Galilee, Samaria and northern Judea declaring orthodox Jewish independence. Judas of Gamala was particularly popular and successful until the Roman army squelched his uprising by destroying whole towns by massacring inhabitants, young and old, male and female. Judas was captured and crucified in 6BC. Brutal Roman raids and public executions turned many citizens against the movement so supporters went underground and operated by stealth. Adherents were renowned for their clever assassinations of Roman soldiers, Temple dignitaries, and Publicans. They became popularly known as dagger men.

Prospective leaders of movements that came out of Galilee were highly suspect because of the history of radical uprisings that arose from the area. Ill-conceived and miscalculated efforts often caused problems that grieved innocent bystanders who got caught up in the inevitable Roman counter insurgencies. Hence, a famous quote that reflected the sentiment of most Jews of the day, "Can any good arise out of Nazareth?" It was in this environment that synagogues began springing up. Citizens of Israel valued their history, honored God, and respected the Temple, but archeology has revealed that virtually everyone conceded the establishment was blatantly corrupt and incompetent. Social, economic, and geographical factions developed. Political and religious divisions deepened. And nobody was watching out for the common folks.

By law and custom a quorum of ten people could convene Beit Midrash for Torah study. Every local village had a Beit Kinesset, or place of gathering. Highly educated insightful men, called rabbis, rose up to teach Torah and mentoring moved out of the Temple and into the public. A formal system of tutoring and personal development caught on and gripped the nation. Structures were built to accommodate teaching, community meetings, and celebrations. Over time a template developed with bench seating along the walls, an elevated platform, and an entrance facing Jerusalem. Every facility had one thing in common. There had to be a permanent mikvah, or what we would call a baptistery, built into the building or dug into the ground outside.

A mikvah held 200 gallons of rainwater that was gathered and siphoned into the tub, or transported under specific regulations. Every community had access to a mikvah, and dozens of them conveniently dotted the landscape at the southern main entrance to the Temple grounds in Jerusalem. Baptism, or periodic ritualistic cleansing, accompanied every major feast or Jewish celebration. Officiating priests needed to be purified before entering the Temple. Any priest could baptize, and some specialized in baptizing. The world's natural bodies of water were deemed preferable when available. Oceans, rivers, wells, and spring-fed lakes were mikvahs in their most primal form. They contained waters of divine source and thus, tradition taught, the power to purify.

At the onset of the first century the people of Israel were disappointed, disillusioned, and disgusted with their lot. Many were pessimistic, but a great many were hopeful. Their study of the Torah, and their adherence to the faith of their forefathers, assured them that God had something better in store for people who could cling to his ways and persevere through adversity. Devout Jews genuinely expected God to intercede again on their behalf at any time. They longed for Messiah to come.

6

A Plan Comes Together

In the Gospel that bears his name, Luke wrote that an elderly priest by the name of Zachariah from the clan of Abijah burned incense in the Temple while a crowd of people waited outside and prayed. The Old Testament book of 1st Chronicles lists the shifts that were originally assigned to Temple duty throughout the year. King David divided priestly families into units. Beginning Nisan 1, the Jewish New Year, these units rotated, serving for one week apiece. Abijah, the unit Zachariah was born into, had the eighth shift. Nisan corresponds to late March and early April on the Julian calendar. That means Zachariah would have served in June, and again in December.

Josephus, the first-century Jewish historian was of the lineage of the priestly course of Jehoiarib, the first unit, so he knew what he was writing about. "When David had separated the priests from them, he found of these priests twenty-four courses, sixteen of the house of Eleazar and eight of that of Ithamar. And he ordained that each course should minister to God for eight days, from Sabbath to Sabbath. Thus were the courses distributed by lot in the presence of David, his high priests Zadok and Abiathar, and all of the rulers. That course which came up first was written down as the first, and accordingly the second, and so on to the twenty-fourth; and this partition hath remained to this day."

With only twenty-four courses, each course was required to work twice a year, leaving three extra weeks on the 354 day Jewish lunar calendar. Leap years periodically added a full 30 day month. The holiday celebrations of Passover, Pentecost, and Tabernacles, during which all the courses were required to serve, made up the three extra weeks. Each unit worked five weeks out of the year; two in their specific courses and three during the holiest feast seasons.

If Zachariah performed rituals in the courtyard, the inner court, or the chamber called the Holy Place, one of two pre-assigned assistant priests could have joined to aid or check on him while he burned incense. The scenario given by Luke poses problems because no one could access Zachariah as he "took an inordinate amount of time offering incense while the people waited outside and prayed." Because of Zachariah's heritage and station another possibility also looms large.

Once a year, every year, Jews gathered in Jerusalem for a solemn assembly that is still called Yom Kippur, or Day of Atonement. On that day, and that day only, the Head Priest entered alone into a fifteen by fifteen by fifteen foot chamber called the Holy of Holies at the heart of the Temple to burn incense and sprinkle the blood of a sacrificial male lamb on the Ark of the Covenant.

The room was unfurnished except for the Ark and the table it sat on. Inside the ornate gold plated acacia wood chest were Aaron's staff, Moses' tablets of the law, and a golden pot filled with manna, or miracle bread from the Exodus. The Head Priest bathed in a mikvah and put on special clean robes before he proceeded into the sacred cubicle behind the thick heavy seemless curtain that served as the only barrier to "God's presence". Thousands silently waited outside and prayed.

If the Head Priest was impure, or his offering was unacceptable, tradition held that God would smite him where he stood. A new rope was tied around his ankle in case those outside needed to pull his corpse out from under the veil. No one could reenter the chamber until a new Head Priest was anointed. The Bible says that Zachariah burned incense in the Temple while a great crowd solemnly waited outside and prayed. By heritage, experience and tenure Zachariah was certainly qualified to be Head Priest. Since we don't have a dependable list of Head Priests and when they served, and we can't confidently confirm what he was doing, the event remains clouded in mystery.

We can't know whether Zachariah was chief priest over a few million people, or served directly under that special one. He was, nonetheless, a very high ranking priest and was considered one of the most highly regarded and universally trusted figures of his day. We are told that he was terribly reverent and faithful. We also know he was a descendant of Levi, Aaron, and Abijah and that his wife, Elizabeth, was the daughter of an esteemed priest who carried Aaron's lineage through Zadok. Zachariah and Elizabeth had no children after decades of marriage. That was both unusual and disgraceful in Hebrew culture. It was particularly disheartening because of the impeccable pedigree a son of such a union would enjoy at a time when Israel was starving for a well-documented righteous leader.

If I said that a space ship hovered above the Temple and aliens beamed down to address Zachariah, a large portion of readers would naively keep reading to see what they proposed. If I said ghosts of past ancestors filled the room and spoke with him, the story would assume yet greater credibility for some. If I said a wizard watched Zachariah in the Temple through a stagnant pond and spoke to him, many modern readers wouldn't give it a second thought.

Instead, the Bible asserts God's direct intervention into a physical world he created from nothing. A number of people have difficulty with that, even though this revelation conveys the culmination of

God's plan for humanity on Earth that was established in the initial verses of Genesis. Supernatural elements reportedly exploded in the region over the next three decades according to the texts. God communicated with men in many forms, and now he was about to pay his Earth a personal visit.

Zachariah was terrified by the angelic form that appeared before him. "Don't worry," God's messenger conveyed, "the Lord knows your untainted heart's desire." According to the Bible, Zachariah spent an unusual amount of time at the altar. Minutes seemed like hours as the hushed crowd waited outside and wondered what was going on, and why it was taking so long. "You're aged wife will have a son," the angel declared, "and you will name him John. In accordance with the holy scriptures that forecast his arrival, your son will pave the way for Messiah to address his people." That Zachariah questioned his experience was to be expected. When he openly expressed disbelief the angel gave him a clear omen. "You can question the Lord's sovereignty in such a matter, but you will have nothing to say about it."

At last, Zachariah emerged from the chamber, pail and trembling to offer the customary public blessing and closing benediction. The crowd knew something very unusual happened, because Zachariah couldn't speak. He tried to express himself as best he could with hand gestures. The rapt crowd was fascinated. They disbanded and went home following Zachariah's awkward blessing and benediction.

Still mute, Zachariah and his wife sought seclusion insolated among family and close friends in their home village of Juttah, five miles south of Hebron in the hill country of Judea along the Bethlehem Road. Five months passed before Elizabeth was confirmed pregnant. She was beside herself. The couple moved back to Ein Karem, an upper class district of Jerusalem, and Elizabeth proudly walked the steep public paths then laden with lush fauna and fruit trees where other wealthy clerics lived.

About a month before she was due, Elizabeth answered a knock at her door. Her young niece, the daughter of her sister Anna and her brother-in-law Joachim who lived at Nazareth in Galilee paid her a call. The Bible recounts Mary's recollection that upon their opening exchange Elizabeth laughed and shared that the baby in her womb leapt and kicked with joy.

Mary stayed a couple of weeks and left when the baby was born. Elizabeth presented her newborn son and told those who gathered that his name was Yochanan, or John. Hebrew tradition dictated that a son carry the name of a respected relative, but no one in either parent's lineage was ever named John. Zachariah asked for a tablet and as soon as he confirmed in writing that he was directed by God to name the boy John, his voice returned and he publicly exalted the sovereign Lord he had questioned.

Zachariah devoted himself to raising his son with divine purpose. God arranged John's unique heritage, a perfectly credentialed priest in a confused nation at a precarious time. God orchestrated the rise and fall of nations that established a common currency and a universal language in a chaotic world. He provided a peaceful generation in the midst of suppressed violent aggression. And he provided the most excellent Torah training a young boy who was to pave the way for Messiah could ever have received.

7

Mary and Joseph

Six months after the angel materialized before Zachariah in the Temple, he appeared to a teenaged girl in Nazareth, Galilee, eighty miles away. "Hello, fortunate young lady," came the pleasant greeting as Mary froze in place. "Don't worry," he reassured her. "I have great news for you." When the angel shared that Mary was going to have a baby, and that the baby was destined to claim the crown of his great ancestor King David and reign over Israel, and would be regarded more reverently and become more well-known than any world leader in history, she nearly fainted.

"How can that be?" She questioned. "I'm a virgin. I've never had a sexual encounter." The angel explained that the child she would conceive only needed her X chromosome to attain every physical attribute and trait he would need to be fully human. Then he shocked her by adding that the Y chromosome would be supernaturally embedded by the eternal Spirit of Holiness that would manifest God on Earth in human form. It made sense to Mary, and she innocently acquiesced without reservation to become an instrument of the God she reverently worshipped and sought to serve all her young life. "I am at my Lord's disposal," she humbly submitted.

Then the angel appeared to a man named Joseph who was so focused in his prayer that he became entranced. God's messenger revealed that the young girl across town that he was formally obligated to marry was already pregnant though they hadn't consummated the marriage. The clear message was that the child was the result of a divine intervention, but with no frame of reference Joseph couldn't comprehend it.

When Joseph came to, he pondered what happened and tried to figure it out. Because he was so devout and Bible literate he was open to a miracle birth as foreshadowed by Abraham and Sarah when they had Isaac, or when Elkanah and Hannah conceived the great prophet Samuel at a very old age. Joseph had also heard the joyous news regarding Mary's kinfolk, Zachariah and Elizabeth. However, all of those pregnancies were sanctioned in the context of years of marriage. Matters of faith always seem more complicated and difficult for someone who has to bear the brunt of social stigma.

Joseph confirmed that Mary was pregnant and considered putting the marriage off, or sending her away to avoid the embarrassment of a public stoning. He was a good man who worked hard to earn a reputation for pious moral character, yet it was incumbent upon him to protect Mary. He desperately wanted to do the right thing, but he was confused and bewildered.

The angel returned and clarified the situation. Joseph's heritage was no accident. His lineage uniquely allowed him to assert his inheritance and claim the throne of David through Solomon to whom it passed. Mary's link to David was through Solomon's brother, Nathan. Joseph was able to see his place in God's enduring scheme on Earth. A just man, committed to righteousness, and willing to make an uncomfortable, unconventional, and quite risky stand for God, Joseph agreed to go through with the marriage and lend his credentials to Mary's child as his adopted first son.

Dozens of very specific Old Testament prophecies already framed the incarnation of a Jewish Messiah. The nation's savior would be a descendant of King David, from the root of Jesse. He would be born of a virgin. He would be a prophet on the scale of Moses the lawgiver. He would be a descendant of Abraham the Semite through Isaac, not Ishmael. He would come through Jacob, not Esau. He would be the seed of a woman, yet every other man was referred to in scripture as the seed of his father.

Messiah would be a priest like Melchizedek, who also reigned as king and maintained peace in the midst of warring worldly tribes. Melchizedek preceded Levi, Aaron, and Zadok. His origin and his death were, and remain, clouded in mystery. Messiah would inherit the scepter of Judah that would not depart until Shiloh arrived, where Shiloh is a reference to a place of Shalom, which means peace in Hebrew. Judah was not Israel's firstborn who would ordinarily obtain the birthright to a double portion of property and ascend to lead the clan. Judah was not Israel's favorite son, on whom he bequeathed a double portion by skipping a generation and adopting his grandsons as sons. And Judah was not the son upon whom Israel established the priesthood for the nation. But Judah's was the line on whom his father Jacob clearly prophesied that once the crown, a regal vestment, was planted, it would never depart.

Moses was from Levi. Joshua was from Ephraim. Gideon was from Manasseh. Samson was from Dan. Samuel was from Ephraim. Saul was from Benjamin. But David was from the lineage of Judah. Jeroboam from the clan of Ephraim became king of the northern tribes of Israel that fell into obscurity. Only Solomon's son Rehoboam's line, from the house of David, coupled with Solomon's brother Nathan's line could stand up to the scrutiny of Temple records that had been meticulously preserved over hundreds of years. The scepter had not passed from Judah, but no true king of Judah's lineage reigned over Israel.

According to prophecy, Messiah had to enter the Temple and teach there. So it had to physically exist and be operating, which was intermittent throughout history. Messiah would perform many miracles and teach in parables, employing illustrations and riddles. Some issues were clear to Joseph, some he could not yet have known. But two things must have shaken him at his core. Isaiah and Malachi both prophesied that Messiah would be introduced by a highly credentialed priest whom the Jews would equate with Elijah, proclaiming his advent in the wilderness. Joseph knew about John.

On top of that, Micah prophesied the Messiah would be born in a city named Bethlehem; specifically Bethlehem that used to be called Ephrata. That's were Boaz was from. That's where Jesse and David were born. A few months prior to his inexplicable confrontation with an angel, Joseph happened to receive a one year advance notice that the Caesar of Rome was summoning his clan to Bethlehem for a tax enrollment. The timing was extraordinary.

It may be hard to reconcile the concept of a person's free will with such evidence that events are predestined. But if Joseph had elected not to listen to and comply with the will of God as he understood it, Messiah was coming anyway. That much was inalterably predetermined.

8

Jesus' Birth and Infancy

The trip from Nazareth to Bethlehem was over ninety miles and took up to six days by foot under ordinary circumstances. Mary was nine months pregnant so even if she rode a donkey, which the Bible doesn't specify, it probably took longer. Israel was relatively safe and Roman soldiers were dispatched to monitor trade routes in order to accommodate and protect census travelers.

Caesar Augustus scheduled his national tax census for September, the month of Tabernacles, a harvest festival during which people live in booths, or tents, for a week. At the end of the harvest season people could more easily travel to their original family homesteads. The cool dry weather was conducive, and citizens had accumulated virtually all the revenue they would bring in for the current year.

Over a hundred thousand people converged on a village of less than 30,000. By the time Joseph and Mary arrived at Bethlehem there were no vacant rooms. The couple most likely stayed with family. Virtually everyone who made the trip was related somehow. The Greek word kataluma, translated "inn" in the Bible, simply meant a shelter or abode that could accommodate guests. The baby was dropping and Mary was going to give birth at any time.

Their hosts probably had a typical house structure where domesticated animals were brought into an enclosed courtyard for safekeeping at night. The house proper would have been stationed on an elevated platform and stairs blocked the animals out. Or, they may have stayed in a cave barn where people herded livestock and penned them overnight. Ironically, they could have been offered space in a holding area for yearling lambs that were set aside specifically for future sacrifice.

Mary probably had a semblance of privacy amidst the crowd, but her accommodations were not pleasant. If it were actually during Tabernacles they would have been in a booth or tent. At least she wasn't in an open pasture, or a crowded makeshift roadside camp like other late arrivals. The noise and smell of anxious animals kept the weary people awake. The flurry of human activity while Mary gave birth kept the curious animals awake.

Joseph acted as his bride's midwife, swaddled her baby tightly in linen strips as was the custom, then laid him on a manger. What we know as a feed trough did not exist in Israel. Joseph actually laid the infant on a feeding ledge or food shelf. Translated from Greek to Aramaic to Hebrew and back into English it might have been referred to appropriately as a "bread table" in common vernacular.

A baby sweetly cooed, a father proudly grinned, a mother finally relaxed, and angels joyously sang. Nearby shepherds tended their flocks in a field, perhaps the very field that Ruth gleaned from, or one where David slayed a fox, a mountain lion, or a snake with his slingshot. In the cool of the night as the shepherds lay about, marveling at the abundant stars in the clear dark sky, they experienced a curious apparition. Angelic beings materialized all around them.

"Hail," a spokesman announced, "We have come to announce that a child was born in the city of David today. The governance of the entire human race rests upon him alone. He will grow to be a mighty king who will save his people from their destructive ways. He has come to establish relationships and restore fellowship with people on Earth. Consider him Emanuel, which means God among us."

The angels jubilantly shared that the young king was sleeping peacefully at the edge of town. And then they were gone. A group of shepherds ran toward the village, determined to check out what they heard from the divine messengers. Not unlike Aaron venturing into the Sinai dessert and encountering Moses, the shepherds were providentially directed to their destination. By the time they found Mary and Joseph with the baby, a crowd had already gathered round. The shepherds shared their story with those who were there. Everyone marveled, and Mary coveted the memory of the event she later shared with Luke, the gospel writer, forty years later. That morning the shepherds returned to their field, amazed that everything was just like it had been described to them.

When Jesus was eight days old, Mary and Joseph walked to Jerusalem six miles north to have him circumcised in the Temple and officially register the birth. They named him Jesus as they had been instructed. The name, derived from Yeshua in the Hebrew tongue, meant God's salvation. More accurately, it originally meant God has saved us, God is saving us, and God will save us. The term is not time sensitive so it covers all tenses.

Simeon, the righteous old priest that facilitated the initiation ritual took Jesus into his arms and proclaimed, "Lord, let me now depart this world in peace. I have beheld that which I have desired to see; a light to enlighten the gentiles, and the glory of your people, Israel." Simeon gave the parents his blessing and told Mary her son was destined to fall and rise again for the sake of God's people. "He is destined for a miracle that will remain controversial and compel people to examine their true convictions." Then he looked at Jesus and added, "Your heart will be pieced too."

Joseph and Mary were still reeling from what they heard when an eighty eight year old widow named Anna approached. Her husband had been a priest and she now lived on the Temple grounds where she interceded in prayer for people all day every day. She approached and simply said, "Thank the Lord. This child will one day deliver all those in Jerusalem who anticipate a redeemer."

Joseph and Mary took up residence among their relatives in Bethlehem. Going back to Nazareth now would be much more difficult, and a good carpenter, someone who could build with wood and stone, was always in demand in a growing Jewish community.

9

Curious Star

The Bible opens with a condensed amalgamation of the roots of science, theology, history, philosophy and conjecture. At a point something undeniably real began to unfold and develop from an absolute void through a state of chaotic flux to an orderly structure. "In the beginning God created the heavens and the earth. And the earth was without form and void, and darkness was upon the face of the deep. And the Spirit of God moved upon the face of the waters. And God said, 'Let there be light...'" Since then, the laws of thermodynamics have remained in place and E has equaled MC^2.

On the fourth day, or stage of creation, God said, "Let there be lights in the firmament of the heaven to divide the day from the night. And let them be for signs, and for seasons, and for days and years." The clear assertion from this earliest of literary efforts is that time is not random, it is ordered. It was set up to be established, manageable, and dependable. This obvious truth allows intelligent beings that were not random occurrences but intentional creatures to inspect, analyze, understand, and even predict great mysteries of the unreachable universe we occupy.

We can now reduce any tangible object. A solid block of coal chipped into solid fragments and pulverized into solid particles of solid dust turns out to be composed of porous molecules that are constituted of porous atoms that are simply animated protons, neutrons, and electrons that are only perceptible images projected by quarks. Everything we call matter is nothing but infinitesimal units of energy that are established, manageable, and dependable, just like sound waves and light waves. "God said (sound waves), let there be light (light waves), and it (material composition) was so."

We strive to dissect, define and harness time, space, matter, and energy, but modern science hasn't yet got a clue as to what's behind the force that initiated their existence and holds them together. Around 940 BC, the writer of Ecclesiastes in the Bible concluded, "all is vanity". Everything men consider tangible substance lacks a firm tangible foundation. When absolute truth is ultimately revealed Bible believers expect to find "I am" to be the sole source of "what is".

The vast empty seemingly meaningless firmament above is so structured and orderly that computer generated models can accurately roll back the astronomical clock and give us a snapshot of stars and planets as they appeared from different points on Earth at any given moment eons in the past. When Cyrus sponsored Ezra's return to Israel with 40,000 Jews, hundreds of thousands of their kinfolk stayed behind. The Bible lists whole families of Levite priests that stayed to teach, train, and lead in worship. Persia was known to be an advanced scientific community where magi, or astronomers, were among the most celebrated figures of their time.

Hundreds of years passed. Imagine a Jewish descendant of a liberated slave doing any of a number of tasks that would put him within earshot of a couple of magi discussing their rooftop observations in September of 5 BC. Jupiter, the regal planet, so called by early astrological fraternities in Babylonia, Persia, Egypt, and distant China, entered into a triple conjunction with Regulus, the bright royal star, in the orbit of Saturn, the planet of authority, so designated because of its rings, in the constellation of Leo, the Lion. Then the sun rose in Virgo, the virgin.

The International Society for Astronomical Research, National Aeronautics and Space Administration, planetariums worldwide, recent international space exploration, and numerous independent sources have aligned to explain and confirm the Bible. If you are a Christian looking to bolster your faith or acquire confidence in your testimony, or an agnostic seriously questioning the Biblical narrative, you need to look up Bethlehem Star on the Internet. The king of planets lined up with the king of stars. It seemed to reverse its course as it looped around and did it again. Then it proceeded back on its course and did it again. It did so in the house of the Lion. Then the Sun came forth from the virgin and light overcame the darkness. Astronomers with no Biblical point of reference simply call it a star dance.

Israel had twelve sons who had families that became tribes. Let's revisit Jacob's deathbed blessing on his son Judah over three thousand years ago. "You are a lion's cub, O Judah. You return from the prey, my son. He crouches like a lion and lies down like a lioness. Who dares to rouse him? The scepter will not depart from Judah, nor the ruler's staff from between his feet, until it comes to whom it belongs and the obedience of the nations is his."

Any devout Jew who was nominally familiar with established history and prophecy and was looking for Messiah at the onset of the first century would have known exactly why royalty and power were ascending in Judah. The testimony of an excited Jewish lad who studied Tanach (Jewish Bible) enough to recite large sections of it would be very convincing. The magi set out on a road trip. Knowing little more than that the heavens proclaimed a new king had come to reign over Israel, and that he was destined to rule the world, the magi headed for Jerusalem, the capital of Judea. Upon their arrival they went to the governor's office to inquire, "Where is he that is born to be 'King of the Jews'?"

That was not something Herod the Great wanted to hear. King of the Jews was the title Caesar gave him three decades earlier. Herod was seething, but outwardly remained charming for his unsuspecting guests. He called for the priests and scribes and scholars of Israel to ask if the wise men from the East might be onto something. He learned that Micah prophesied hundreds of years before, "And you, Bethlehem Ephrata in the land of Judea are not insignificant among the principalities of Judah. From you shall come a governor that will rule my people, Israel."

Herod served a banquet and sent the magi on their way. He deceitfully directed them to come back on their way home and let him know where they found the little king so he could look him up and pay his respect as well. The caravan from Persian Babylonia carried gold, myrrh and frankincense that the foreign aristocrats entrusted to Joseph on behalf of the infant king when they found him. Then, knowing how much commotion the magi stirred up and that they couldn't live inconspicuously anymore, Joseph had more than a hunch he needed to move his family to Egypt where they would be safe.

When weeks passed and the magi didn't return, Herod got suspicious and threw a royal tantrum. He calculated the age of the child based on what the magi and the Jewish scholars told him, and ordered that every male child in the vicinity of Bethlehem under the age of three be put to the sword. That too inadvertently fulfilled Jeremiah's prophesy, "A great cry was heard in Ramah; Rachael weeping for her children. But she cannot be comforted. They have all perished."

Jacob's wife Rachael bore Joseph, who had Ephraim and Manasseh in Egypt. She died giving birth to Benjamin on the way to Bethlehem and was buried in a cave at Ramah. The little town of Bethlehem, meaning house of bread, was called Ephratah, meaning fruitful, by Hebrews at the time. All Rachael's babies in the area were annihilated. One of Leah's children, a descendant of Judah, escaped.

When the Jewish Kingdom split following Solomon's reign, his son Rehoboam presided over the southern kingdom of Judah. Rehoboam's cousin, Jeroboam of the tribe of Joseph's son Ephraim, assumed the throne over the ten tribes of the northern kingdom of Israel. Ephraim was the rebellious descendant clan of Rachael and upon their massacre Rachael was surely "turning over in her grave". It was predicted centuries before it happened.

The slaughter of young Jewish boys in the region was reprehensible, but thorough. Mothers wailed and Jews throughout the kingdom objected, but Herod, who routinely killed his own sons to keep the throne, heard nothing more about another Jewish king for as long as he lived. Archeological records divulge that Herod the Great almost certainly did not live through another year.

10

Jesus' Childhood

Joseph, Mary and young Jesus fled to Egypt, the nation that insulated and nurtured Abraham, Isaac, Jacob, and ultimately the entire nation of Israel through trying formative times. Eight centuries earlier the prophet Hosea envisioned God beckoning his son out of Egypt. After a few years living in exile Joseph heard that Herod died, and felt that it was finally safe to bring his family home.

As they entered the province of Judea they learned that Herod's wicked son, Archelaus, occupied his father's throne. So they passed through Bethlehem and took the road that went through Bethany a few miles east of Jerusalem, continuing on to the city of Nazareth in the province of Galilee. That not only took them over the mountains a safe distance beyond the capital, it fulfilled Isaiah's prophecy that Messiah would be a Nazarene.

Joseph was a carpenter and stone mason so he was able to make a good living and raise a family in Nazareth, where Mary grew up. The Bible reveals that Jesus had four brothers and several sisters. His half-brothers, considering Joseph to be their actual biological father, were James, Joseph, Judas, and Simon. One of his sisters was named Salome. Most, if not all, of the siblings were born in Nazareth after Jesus was at least five years old.

According to cultural norms, Joseph would have taught Jesus his trade, and no doubt they spent hours working on projects together. Joseph also ensured that Jesus got a proper Jewish education. All children were home schooled until they were five years old. Most Jewish children learned basic reading skills at home, and most learned to write. There were twenty two letters in the Hebrew alphabet, called the alefbet because alef and bet were the first two letters. There were no vowels and the familiar dots and dashes were probably added after the third century.

Nbdy hd dffclty lrnng Hbrw bcs thy ddnt hv vwls.

Hebrew was written and read right to left from top to bottom. All twenty two letters also represented numbers. Alef (echad) was 1, bet (shtayim) was 2, gimmel (shalosh) was 3, and dalet (arba) was 4. The tenth letter, yod (esser), was 10. Kaf, the eleventh letter (esra echad) started at 20 rising by 10 to the nineteenth which was 100. Then the last three corresponded to 200, 300 and 400. As an example: TRYB, or Tav + Reish + Yod + Bet, added up to 612.

Jewish custom was to wake up and say a morning prayer before rising. Devout Jewish men wore tefillin, or phylacteries, strapped on their chest, arm, or head. Prayers and scriptures were stuffed into these small pouches and committed to memory. Almost every Jew committed large blocks of the Torah to memory. Rote prayers and major passages of Torah were easily recited verbatim by almost every member of a normal Jewish community.

Boys and girls attended separate classes at beit midrash, usually convened at a local synagogue, from the ages of five to eleven. Thereafter, boys who were particularly good students were invited to continue studying under an assigned rabbi. Some students, called talmidim, attached themselves to a rabbi for life, or until there was nothing more that particular rabbi could teach them. The goal of every good rabbi was to reproduce himself in pupils who would carry his knowledge and understanding to an even higher level. John, who became the Baptizer, was mentored by his father Zachariah and had the benefit of being surrounded by Zachariah's elite peers. By the time of his bar mitzvah that formally ushered him into manhood within his clan when he reached puberty, John was perhaps the greatest priestly prodigy Israel had seen in many generations.

Six months younger than his cousin, Jesus enjoyed playing and studying with John when the family came to Jerusalem for holiday feasts. Since Joseph and Mary were devout they probably made the pilgrimage several times a year. On Passover when Jesus and John were twelve or thirteen years old, they stayed in the Temple to listen in on high ranking priests' discussions after an assembly. Mary and Joseph left for Nazareth in a caravan assuming Jesus was in the custody of one of his many cousins or close family friends. They only discovered that Jesus missed the caravan when they stopped for the night. The next day they backtracked and found Jesus in the Temple the following morning after searching for him all over town.

Had Jesus not been Zachariah's nephew there is no way he would have been allowed to sit in such an assembly. Notwithstanding, if he listened politely, he still would not have been allowed to address the distinguished elder clerics while they were in session. When Mary and Joseph saw him in their midst they were taken aback. The priests were drilling him and marveled at his knowledge and insight. He was already able to discuss and relate Torah at or near their level.

When his mother expressed that she and Joseph had been worried about him and searched for him all over town, he humbly replied, "I figured you would know that I would be here at the Temple pursuing my father's business," an honest and very revealing response. Knowing his nature and interest, the Temple should have been the first place they looked.

The Bible discloses that Jesus excused himself, rejoined his father and mother, to whom he was always respectful and submissive, and returned to Galilee where, "he grew in wisdom and stature, and in favor with God and man." Under his parents' excellent supervision Jesus continued to develop mentally, physically, spiritually, and socially.

Not much more is known of Jesus' upbringing beyond that momentous occasion. But he was strategically and providentially placed in Joseph and Mary's household and availed of Zachariah's tutelage by design for a purpose. Both John and Jesus listened to their parents and understood their special destiny.

Part 2

Jesus' Ministry

11

Reunion at the River

No one can serve in the House of Representatives until he is 25 years old, or become a US Senator before he turns 30. There is no exception for education, experience, or pedigree. The rules don't bend to knowledge or desire. Likewise, the eighth chapter of Numbers stipulates that the descendants of Levi had to be at least 25 years old to serve in the Temple and were forced to retire when they reached 50. Certain offices and duties, including service on the High Court, were legally restricted to priests who were 30 and older. The prevalent view of 70 elderly clerics presiding over the Sanhedrin is absolutely wrong, though many highly regarded Jewish "elders" remained active as respected scholars and valued consultants.

Zachariah and Elizabeth were relatively old when John the Baptist was born. What we know from Holy Scriptures and extra-biblical sources indicates that Zachariah, Elizabeth, and Jesus' father Joseph died while their sons were adolescents or young adults. The biblical context pits Jesus and John contending with powerful dignitaries and seasoned national leaders who were in their thirties and forties.

However, John was not welcomed in the established seat of national power. Those with authority and influence were too vested to allow a potentially disruptive force access to their institutions. The power brokers on the inside closed the door and locked it shut. Annas, the Head Priest, violated protocol in order to keep John, an advocate for righteousness, out of the halls of power. Annas lobbied for his son-in-law, Caiaphas, to replace him before he had to step aside, and packed the High Court with young cronies of his own choosing. Besides being immoral and unethical, it was arguably criminal. Yet, when a nation's rulers instigate a crime then formally validate their own action with a new law or sanction, government standing makes their misdeed technically legal.

It might be years before John could be considered for a seat on the bench. Further, he would have a hard time penetrating establishment ranks. If he got in, he would face a resistant block that would seek to silence him on every point he sought to raise. John took his ministry to the wilderness of humanity. His popularity soared when he found his platform among the common folks.

John took off his priestly garments and dressed like everyone else. It was late autumn. He put on a camel hair coat and cinched it with a leather belt. He didn't need the vestments. They were an uncomfortable distraction for him and the people he wanted to get to know and help. He didn't care to sit at the head table and eat delicacies like other priests. Carob trees were abundant. Their hard brown pods filled with seeds rattled in the breeze and sounded like locusts. John was content to join the peasants and spread locust jam and honey over a piece of bread. Imagine a high ranking official in our day donning a denim jacket and sitting down with common folks to eat peanut butter and jelly sandwiches. The masses paid homage to the other priests, but they adored John and flocked to him.

John could pass for a regular guy, but his confident demeanor separated and elevated him. Whether he employed the sophisticated elegance of the high court's Hebrew, earthy Greek, or Aramaic slang used by poor peasants, he commanded attention and respect when he spoke. He didn't mince words in private conversations or public declarations. Large crowds followed him out of the city to the banks of the storied Jordan River. The gist of his message was "Straighten up, or pay a price for your crooked ways." He was relentless in advocating for repentance to righteous God honoring behavior. He often ended his public discourses with an invitation to participate in the ritual cleansing of baptism. In fact, he became widely known for it and adopted the moniker, "John the Baptist". When folks mentioned the Baptizer, everyone knew who they were referring to.

One day while John was preaching and baptizing at the Jordan River, Jesus approached on the opposite bank. John recognized him and uttered, "Look, the lamb of God whose personal sacrifice will at last resolve the issue of human sin." The cousins, who hadn't seen each other in years, smiled and waded into the water. Jesus, now also in his thirties, asked John to baptize him and pointed out that it was time for him to be anointed. John was aware of the moment. He studied the holy scrolls under the guidance of his father, Zachariah, and knew the conditions of both births and the convergence of their destinies.

"It would be more fitting that you should baptize me," John observed, conceding the relative authority vested in each of them according to the scriptures both of them drank in and absorbed.

"Do what has to be done in order to officially sanction me according to our rules and regulations," Jesus admonished him. So John baptized Jesus and declared that he was the one upon whom God's spirit descended. John had envisioned the occasion many times. He delighted in his task, but their time together was short. Jesus was drawn into the mountains to fast and pray in solitude for forty days. He wrestled with his fate as Jacob had wrestled at Peniel. There and then, Jesus irrevocably committed to thoroughly relinquish his own will in order to fulfill scripture and abide by every law and unction of God.

Jesus was a normal man, but the blood that coursed through his human veins was different. His mother and father, and even his uncle, reminded him that God was his true father. There was an eternal purpose for his birth on Earth. The scriptures he consumed held the key. The Bible had been his steady diet. He gobbled up the scriptures and digested them. They were his heart's desire and the fabric of his being. He was the walking, talking, animated word of God.

Jesus hiked into the foreboding mountains to face down the devil that was his natural nemesis. He alone, in whom God's spirit dwelled, could save humanity from the fate imposed on the world by man's first willful excursion into sin. Satan appealed to Jesus' vanity, attacked his logic, and lured him with physical gratification and sensual pleasure. Jesus knew then that he was Messiah, the Christ. He prevailed and resolved to finish the course set before him. He was resolute. He understood the stakes.

12

A Wedding at Cana

Jesus came down from the mountain and passed through the Baptist's crowded camp to cross the Jordan River. John was famous. Many people throughout Israel considered him to be the greatest Bible teacher and orator that ever lived. As Jesus passed through their midst John pointed him out to a couple of young men who had attached themselves to him and humbly said, "That's the fellow I called the Lamb of God. My impact will diminish. His will grow. Go, follow him."

With curiosity peaked, Andrew and his cousin John went to check him out. When Jesus noticed them following at a distance he cordially invited them to come along. Andrew was in his early twenties and John was a young teenager. As they reached the vicinity of Capernaum in Galilee, Andrew went to fetch his older brother. Andrew was already convinced that Jesus was the Messiah, or Christ, Israel's promised savior. When Andrew introduced his brother Simon, Jesus, ever cheerful and warm, called him Peter, variously translated throughout the New Testament from Petros in Greek or Cephas (pronounced kay-fas) in Aramaic. It would be like calling someone Rock or Stony. Simon liked the nickname. It stuck and he went by Peter from that time on.

They continued north to Bethsaida where they encountered Philip, a young associate of Andrew, Peter and John. Philip left to invite his friend Nathaniel who was visiting from Cana, saying, "Come meet the one that was written about in the books of the Law and the Prophets." Deeply skeptical, but a very studious well-read Jew, Nathaniel accompanied him. Hardly into their conversation, Nathaniel blurted, "You really are the Son of God. You are the King of Israel foretold in our scriptures!"

Cana was four miles northeast of Nazareth along what is now promoted as the Jesus Hiking Trail. The tourist route winds nearly thirty miles from Nazareth to Capernaum. It made sense for Jesus and Nathaniel to make the daytrip home together. Peter, Andrew, John and Philip tagged along. The timing may have been prompted by a prescheduled wedding at Cana. It would have been customary for them to be invited, especially since historical records indicate that Nathaniel lived in Cana and Jesus was from neighboring Nazareth. Jesus' mother, Mary, was there, so it's likely that Jesus knew the bride or groom.

The groom's family hadn't anticipated such a crowd and Jewish wedding feasts typically lasted at least seven days. Although friends pitched in, Mary pointed out that they were quickly running out of wine. The poor family would suffer terrible humiliation. The celebration would become a laughing stock. Not wanting to draw attention to himself, Jesus advised his mother that wasn't his business. Mary called a few groomsmen over and instructed them to do whatever Jesus told them to do. Then she backed away. Jesus spotted six clay pots that held 30 to 35 gallons of water and were only used to fill a mikvah, or baptistery. That indicates it may have been a priest or rabbi's house.

He directed the men to fill the containers to the brim so that nothing could be added. Then he told them to fill a cup and take it to the master of ceremonies. They were the only ones that handled the water, and the only ones who knew what was going on. When the master of ceremonies drank from the cup, he called the anxious bridegroom to his side and proposed a toast. "Everyone always serves their best wine first at a banquet, then they bring out an inferior vat. But you," he proclaimed with delight, "have waited until now to bring out this excellent wine." Jesus miraculously supplied over a hundred and fifty gallons of the sweetest wine anyone there ever tasted. There was wine left over when the party ended.

The Bible specifically states this was the first occurrence of Jesus publicly engaging in supernatural activity. In his thirties, when normal DNA compels a body to start breaking cells down faster than it can manufacture them, Jesus tapped into the life bearing chromosome that separated him from the rest of humanity. The Holy Spirit that occasioned his conception and indwelled him upon the Baptist's anointing was now unleashed upon the world. Messiah's time had finally come.

The term repentance was addressed earlier. What Christians today mean by repentance doesn't capture the original meaning of "toshuveh", or calibration. Instead of turning around, or turning from something, like bad behavior, repentance is returning "to" something. It is better portrayed as refocusing and redirecting to a perfect standard or an original design. That necessarily "fixes" problems. Jesus and his cousin John called people to genuine repentance. Both denounced people's bad behavior and warned of ill-fated consequences, but they didn't just say, "Stop doing bad things," or, "alter your course." They pointed people back to God as their beacon. Moving away from something without determining your course is called drifting. That's why "repentant Christians" so often falter.

John and Jesus were taught to be in an "attitude of prayer". That meant they always had their internal radars on. Instead of periodically seeking instruction or correction, then grappling to make a course adjustment, they kept their mental radios on and depended on divine guidance moment by moment.

The term baptism is also often misapplied in modern Christian culture. The Greek root word "bapt" is associated with cleansing. Baptidzo indicates immersion, but baptizontes could be spot cleaning, or sprinkling. Baptisma means washing and was customarily illustrated by repeatedly pouring water over an object. The Bible employs at least six variations rendered as baptism, the most striking of which was Jesus describing the "pouring out" of the Holy Spirit over, or onto, his followers.

If a rock is dipped in water, it gets wet but it doesn't necessarily get thoroughly cleansed. A sponge subjected to sprinkling or partially submerged until it retains water may be an equally practical illustration of baptism. Jewish mikvah washing that we now refer to as baptism, denotes bathing. It was intended to illustrate shedding filth accumulated on the body. For cleansing of internal thoughts, motives and intents, Jews still offered the blood of animals on an altar of sacrifice. After thousands of years of futile human effort, that ancient practice was about to change.

13

Cleansing Begins at the Temple

When Jesus and his entourage left Cana to return to Capernaum where Peter and Andrew lived, a great crowd tagged along clamoring to get close and clinging to his every word. They hadn't been there long before it was time to make the pilgrimage to Jerusalem for the Passover holiday. Almost 300,000 people lived in and immediately around Jerusalem. More than that number lived a daytrip away. Over a million people might have made the pilgrimage for a major holiday feast. Jesus made the trip routinely.

When they were young, John and Jesus played on the Temple grounds like a preacher's son and nephew might have the run of a local church. Jesus knew his way around the complex better than most of the priests and scribes did. He was at home in the Temple. Upon his arrival, having recently been baptized and anointed with the same Holy Spirit that initiated his incarnation and orchestrated turning water into wine, Jesus saw the Temple with fresh eyes. Instead of allowing his spirituality to be conformed to the world around him, he aligned his material existence and directed every physical activity according to the Spirit that surged within him.

A crowd pressed to gain entrance to the Temple but couldn't advance because vendor transactions impeded their progress. Instead of bringing "an offering from their flock" as the law stipulated, the clerics amended the law to make worship more convenient for the masses, and more lucrative for themselves. Well-meaning folks who genuinely wanted to pay homage to God and were willing to sacrifice as their religious leaders directed bought blemished animals at abhorrent prices and waited in line to get a priest's blessing. Receipts and animal dung littered the path to the altar. Jesus cringed. He picked up strands of rope that once bound the necks of lambs, goats, and bull calves, and served to lead them to their deaths at the hands of tainted priests. Those who surrounded him saw the fury in his eyes and gave him space as he braided the cords into a short tight whip.

Silence rippled through the sea of frustrated worshippers, eager vendors, and corrupt clerics when Jesus stepped forward and raised his powerful voice, "My father's house was meant to be a place of sanctuary and worship. But you have turned it into a den of thieves." With no further warning or explanation, pilgrims scattered as Jesus advanced on the vendors' booths and cages, rebuking the merchants, releasing their animals, turning the tables on them and releasing their money into the crowd.

Temple guards were dumbfounded. They stood idly by, not drawing their swords or cracking their bigger whips. When high ranking clerics called for Jesus' immediate arrest, guards turned and walked away. "How dare you," the priests chided, calling Jesus a trespasser and accusing him of a crime. "You're disrupting commerce and destroying the Temple," they charged.

They bantered back and forth until Jesus said, "Destroy this temple and I'll have it reconstituted in three days." They had no idea what he was talking about.

"This Temple compound has been under construction for forty-six years. There's no way you could reconstruct it in three days," they responded. They demanded him to document by what authority he engaged in such behavior and addressed them as equals.

Jesus advised them that just as Jonah spent three days buried in the sea before he emerged to testify against Ninevah, he would spend three days buried in the earth before he arose to testify against them. That, he proposed, would be validation enough. They couldn't make sense of what he told them. Years later, when Jesus arose from a grave and his band of followers reflected back on this encounter, it took on great significance when they realized Jesus was using ancient holy scriptures to prophesy his fate and verify his credentials.

That Passover feast marked the beginning of Jesus' popularity and prominence. When the holiday ended and pilgrims returned to their routine existence, Jesus's reputation exploded in every village throughout Israel. Jesus was the people's champion. Many already perceived him as their potential savior, the Christ portrayed in their ancient scrolls.

People flocked to Jesus. He was an honest man in a corrupt culture. He confronted tyrants. He laughed with those who celebrated and wept with those who mourned. He could talk with anyone, anywhere, at any time as long as they were civil, truthful, and open to new perspectives on cherished beliefs.

Despite anything you might have seen or read from a hostile source, Jesus was not driven by carnal impulses but by principles and discipline. Authenticated accepted gospel texts and reliable historical accounts from recognized sources consistently portray Jesus as a man who would forego any personal gratification to live, or die, according to his values. And the one thing he held above all else was pleasing his heavenly father.

Jesus was not married to, and did not have an affair with, Mary Magdalene. He was not attracted to young John the disciple. He did not perform magic tricks to exhibit his deity. And he did not deny, conceal or question his personal identity. The Bible declares at the onset of his ministry Jesus Christ knew who he was and knew his life's mission. He would not risk failure. He would not compromise. He would not leave room for cynics to make a legitimate claim against him. He was brilliant and he fully understood the dire consequences that would be attached to his every word and deed.

14

Night Visitor

As Jesus' celebrity grew among the peasant population, his welcome among the ruling elite diminished. Three decades passed since Jesus' parents brought him to the Temple to be circumcised, registered, and dedicated. Simeon and Anna were long dead, but others who were there at the time might still recall the infant to whom they gave their prophetic blessings.

Jesus' uncle, Zachariah the priest, died too. When he came into power, Annas purged those who aligned with Zachariah's righteous ways from leadership and installed his young son-in-law, Caiaphas, to replace him as Head Priest. Zachariah's son John was inducted into the priesthood, but effectively snubbed by the Sanhedrin. The young prodigies who played in the Temple when they were boys, debated with Jewish luminaries when they were teens, and might have been expected in some circles to lead the nation out of bondage and into greatness again were outcasts.

Nonetheless, two well-trained, highly credentialed men of unassailable character with clear vision who were excellent communicators with an inspiring message who had outstanding leadership skills still drew large followings. The perception of John as a badly groomed radical religious nutcase yelling and wagging his finger at passersby in the desert is totally out of character; as is the idea that Jesus was a total unknown who arose from obscurity and confronted Temple dignitaries he had never met.

John and Jesus were more likely folk heroes who became more and more recognizable and accepted as people gained exposure to them. My mother had a pleasant encounter with a huge recording artist in New York City in the 1950's. He had sold millions of records. A few people gathered round and giggled, but she had no idea who struck up a conversation with her until he walked away and people who had seen him perform mentioned his name.

Jesus criticized pompous priests who liked being recognized and lauded in public. "You enjoy your elevated status," he said on many occasions. "You wear your fancy robes draped with emblems of power and piety in order to be recognized. You expect others to give you seats of honor after you make a grand entrance, drawing everyone's attention. You want to be served first and given the best meals without paying." And he finished his admonition with, "Why can't you be more like John?"

John was clean, wholesome, modest, accommodating, and easy to be around, but he was brutally frank and honest. Powerful disingenuous hypocrites sought to silence or discredit those who unmasked them for perverting what was sacred for the sake of personal gain or promoting an ideology. Herod Agrippa, the governor of Galilee and grandson of Herod the Great, married the young daughter of a foreign king to further his political ambitions. After Herod gained what he wanted, he divorced her and moved in with his brother's wife with whom he was having an affair. John railed against Herod's blatantly irreverent act of indecency to illustrate how bad things had become. Herod had John arrested for disturbing the peace and his vindictive licentious common-law wife orchestrated his beheading.

The Temple was corrupt too, though there were still decent people in positions of influence. One such priest was a Pharisee by the name of Nicodemus. Sadducees dominated the Sanhedrin. Imbedded in materialism and guided by secular intellectualism, they were callous to the notion that an invisible God was directly engaged in the affairs of men on Earth. They held the traditions of their Jewish heritage, but they did not understand, appreciate, or abide by them unless it served their own interests. They had a hard time relating to Jesus, and Jesus struggled to penetrate their thick shells; much like Moses had difficulty dealing with a self-absorbed highly educated worldly pharaoh.

Sadducees prided themselves on morality without religious hangups, and promoted open-mindedness in civic and academic pursuits. Professorial Sadducees determined that fate rested in the minds of men and conjured an image of God that was comfortable and convenient. Pharisees, on the other hand, were still generally more reverent. They were open to spirituality and had a pliable conscience.

Nicodemus was a brilliant scholar who sympathized with Jesus but didn't want to be shunned by his colleagues. He came to Jesus one night under the cover of darkness, so as to not be recognized. Although priests wore the vestments of their office while on duty, they weren't required to dress up on their personal off-duty time. They did that to feed their egos and Jesus constantly called them out for it. Nicodemus came to Jesus incognito, man to man.

Nicodemus was convinced that God sent Jesus into their midst because no one could know, say, and do what was being attributed to him if he were not empowered by God's spirit. "No one enters or executes in God's domain unless he has been born again," Jesus stated bluntly. "Just as a man has to experience a natural birth to enjoy physical life, he has to go through a transition to enter into a spiritual existence."

Nicodemus was confused, so Jesus explained. "You are an accomplished respected religious scholar, but you've missed the crux of the matter. Only one who has been there could fully comprehend the spiritual domain. That would be the son of man, Adam's rightful heir to the paradise that God initially intended. God loved the world so much he gave his only begotten son so that whoever would fully depend on him would not perish, but go on living forever. God didn't send his son into the world to condemn people, but to save them from the condemnation they've brought on themselves."

"Whoever puts his faith in me will not be judged. But those who refuse to trust me remain condemned because they don't yield to my authority so that I can redeem them. Condemnation is based on the fact the world has been enlightened, but some prefer to remain in the dark because they're maligned. Only those who subject themselves to light can see clearly to align themselves with God."

The Bible doesn't reveal an immediate response, but Nicodemus went on to become an advocate for Jesus privately and publicly. His allegiance would later surface, indicating he understood and personally acquiesced. Despite contrary appearances and a constant angry roar of defiance, Jesus had a voice, perhaps several, in the court of secular government. He still does.

15

Twelve Disciples

If bosses looked upon employees as their children there would be a lot better mentoring and a lot less hanky-panky in the work place. If priests, coaches, and supervisors viewed staff and followers as siblings from a mutual father, affection would be genuine, bountiful, and appropriate. Jesus was an exemplary role model. He didn't violate anyone and could not be seduced. He developed and empowered others.

The role of a rabbi was modeling what his talmidim should become. By the end of their time together each talmidi should know what the rabbi knew, reason like the rabbi reasoned, behave like the rabbi behaved, and react like the rabbi would react in a given situation. Jesus chose his team purposefully. We can't know exactly how it happened, but the Bible gives insights. Andrew and John were disciples of the Baptist. That John the Baptist personally referred them to Jesus says a lot. Andrew fetched his brother Simon. The three invited their friend Philip. Philip sought out his friend Nathaniel. Jesus invited John's big brother, James, to join them. The first six were settled, but Jesus needed at least ten to establish a bona fide Jewish "community" to convene beit midrash, or house of study.

At a glance it appears Jesus impulsively invited poor fishermen to quit their jobs to tag along. That's not accurate at all. After Jesus' encounter with six good prospects, and likely after a wedding they attended together at Cana, Jesus started forming his class. It was a demanding and expensive proposition, so it was more complicated than legend has it. When he said, "Come, let's get going," Jesus had contracts in hand. As with people in the Old Testament, those who were passed over or aren't germane to the story weren't named. The rich young ruler who declined Jesus' invitation may fit that category.

Peter, Andrew, James and John were from a wealthy family that operated a fishing business out of Capernaum and Bethsaida, the two major fishing ports on Lake Gennesaret in Galilee. The lake, also known as the Sea of Galilee, was 14 miles long and 7 miles wide. It is still the lowest fresh water lake on Earth and feeds into the Dead Sea 65 miles downstream. The best fishing waters were at the mouth of the Jordan River as it flowed out of cool clear mountain springs from Syria, Lebanon, and Northern Israel; lands more recently considered Muslim, Christian, and Jewish; through Bethsaida.

Capernaum, six miles southwest along the shoreline, was well suited for deep water fishing launches. Fishing was a major source of revenue in first century Israel. James, John, Peter and Andrew, were the heirs of their fathers' lucrative fishing business. Archeology has uncovered that at some point in history "Zebedee and Sons" held a space at the market in Jerusalem, though attachment to this clan cannot yet be confirmed.

Zebedee ran the operation in Bethsaida where James and John were based. Zebedee's brother John ran the operation in Capernaum where Peter and Andrew lived. Jesus often stayed with Peter and his wife when he came to town. Jesus must have negotiated with Zebedee and John, and they must have liked his proposal for such an agreement to be reached. In the Bible Zebedee's wife, Salome, is often seen bringing food and money to the group's camps. She had immediate personal access to Jesus.

Philip's father may have worked for Zebedee and John, or he might have been a friend from a wealthy merchant family. Their friend, Nathaniel, was a young academic from Cana near Nazareth who was able to travel freely. Jesus also needed a good record keeper and Matthew was a certified tax agent. The Bible discloses that Matthew descended from a line of priests described as Alpheus in Aramaic. That would be alpha in Greek, aleph in Hebrew, or the letter "A" in English. Matthew was born and groomed into the Jewish priesthood and grew up among the "A" team. For him to defect was particularly egregious. He was clearly bright, articulate, and knew his Jewish culture, heritage and religion. He may have been disillusioned by corruption he observed in the priesthood and chose what he reasonably figured was in his best secular material interest.

Matthew had a little brother who was described as scrawny. He wasn't as young as John, who was 12-15 when Jesus invited him. Matthew was thrilled to get a shot at redemption and could easily have paid his little brother's tuition. James the Less, or Little James, was particularly astute. He grew up in Matthew's family of priests. Matthew would have been shaken when he found out a Zealot had been invited to join the group. Simon the dagger man had taken a vow to assassinate corrupt clerics, Roman soldiers, oppressive politicians, or tax collectors when he could. Jesus paired them and got them through their "hate issues". Many people don't consider the tension that inherently came with constituting a group of passionate independent young idealists, all of whom exhibited strong leadership qualities.

Much is known of Thomas' life, travels and demise after his association with Jesus, but not much is known about where he came from or how he was chosen. It's interesting that Jesus, early in their relationship, nicknamed him Didymus. The term is usually translated twin, but it also referred to someone who was two-faced, or more interestingly, undecided or "between two opinions".

To round out the group of twelve, there were two named Judas. Jesus referred to one as Thaddeus, which meant soft hearted, but Thaddeus already had a nickname of Lebbeus. Like Hoss, derived from horse, that indicates he was a man of intimidating stature. He was probably what we might call a big sweet teddy bear. Adults feared him, but kids approached him. He made an excellent body-guard. Thaddeus, Simon the Zealot, and Peter often surrounded Jesus in crowds.

Another Judas was called Iscariot possibly indicating where he was from. He was an "outsider" among twelve Galileans. Literally the term Iscariot meant "from Kerrioth", a city ten miles south of Hebron in Judea. Judas was also called the son of Simon, perhaps Simon the leper who was healed by Jesus and ultimately resided in Bethany three miles east of Jerusalem where Lazarus also lived. That Simon may have been the superintendent over constructing Herod's temple complex before he contracted leprosy.

Judas Iscariot's background may be the most intriguing of those Jesus brought into his fold very methodically. Judas was given the roll of treasurer. Contrary to common understanding, tradition indicates that of all the people around Jesus, Judas was the most trusted and dependable. He alone had what would today be recognized as, "power of attorney". His position as "right hand man" is confirmed by the seating at Jesus' last formal supper. If Jesus was going to "put his life" in the hands of any of them, according to cultural standards then and now, Judas would have been that man.

16

Conversation at a Well

Traveling from Jerusalem back to Cana, Jesus and his talmidim took a shortcut through Samaria, north of Judea and southwest of Galilee. Samaria was the land of the old Northern Kingdom where half-breeds and Jews who couldn't produce their ancestral records settled. There was mutual animosity between the pedigreed Jews of the Southern Kingdom and their compromised cousins. Samaritans were not granted access to the Temple and were actually treated worse than alien gentiles when they came to Jerusalem. They mutually avoided each other whenever it was practical.

Knowing he would attract a crowd and cause a commotion, Jesus sent the others into the village of Sychar to buy food and told them to meet him at a popular nearby well that Jacob had dug 2,000 years before. As he waited, Jesus saw a woman approach in the middle of the day. That was unusual because women always drew water in the cool of the morning. It was a social gathering. Women didn't go to wells alone. This woman must have been an outcast among outcasts.

Jesus politely asked her to draw a drink for him from the old well.

From his attire and demeanor she could easily see he was Jewish as opposed to Samaritan. "Why are you asking me?" she inquired. "You people think you're above talking to us." The chip on her shoulder belied the pain in her heart.

"If you knew who I was, you would have engaged me," he grinned. "If you only knew what I could offer, you would have asked for what I've got."

"You don't have anything to draw with or to drink from," she replied. "And this is a very deep well." She pointed out that Jacob, their common ancestor, dug that well, personally drank from it, and provided water for his family and flocks from it. She shrugged when Jesus suggested he had access to something better than "Israel" initially provided.

"Everyone who drinks from this source gets thirsty again," Jesus explained. "Whoever drinks what I've got for them will ingest a pure satisfying ever-flowing river of life."

When she asked how she could get something like that in her life, Jesus told her to go get her husband and come back. She conveyed that she didn't have a husband. "I know," Jesus replied. "You've had five husbands and you're not married to the man you're living with now. I can deal with someone who's honest."

The conversation took a radical turn to religion and she poured her heart out when she realized Jesus somehow seemed to already know everything about her. "Samaritans worship at nearby altars, but Jews insist that Jerusalem is the only place where God accepts sacrifices," she probed.

Jesus told her that men in authority misappropriate religion in order to obtain, control and direct power, prestige, and property. He explained that men tend to make worship a physical endeavor, but God is a spirit. God isn't concerned about settings and rituals. He acknowledges and accepts a person's genuine contrition and devotion. It doesn't matter where or how they worship.

"When Messiah comes, he'll clear all this up for us," she proposed.

"That's exactly who I am," he stated to her amazement.

Just then Jesus' talmidim arrived and approached timidly, not knowing what was going on and concerned that their new friend Jesus, a Jewish man, would strike up a conversation with a Samaritan woman of obvious questionable repute. They asked Jesus if he was hungry and offered some of what they bought. He relayed that his insatiable appetite for doing what his father sent him for had already been addressed.

"Open your eyes and look around," he beckoned. "The fields are ripe for harvesting. Whoever reaps secures the fruit of eternal life. One sows and another reaps, but they can celebrate together. I'm going to send you out to reap a harvest you didn't sow. The groundwork has been laid, the seeds were planted long ago, and you simply have to gather the fruit."

The woman left her bucket and ran into town to tell everyone that would listen that she met a man who looked right through her and seemed to know everything about her. She was convinced he was the Christ. Hundreds of people ventured out to the well and pled with him to stay a while. Over the next couple of days virtually everyone in Sychar became convinced that Jesus was, in fact, the promised Messiah foretold in the scriptures.

Jesus toured Samaria, Galilee, and Judea drawing large crowds everywhere he went. His fame spread as he taught in synagogues throughout the country, fulfilling Isaiah's prophesy, "In Zebulun and Naphtali, along the coast beyond the Jordan in Galilee where the gentiles live, people who lived in the dark were confronted with great enlightenment. A light dawned on those who dwelled in the shadow of death." The Bible says from that time Jesus proclaimed, "The time has arrived and the kingdom of God is at hand. Believe the good news and reorient your life to it."

Don't think for a minute that Jesus did not know from before the onset of his formal priesthood exactly who he was and why he was born. Those who say or write that Jesus didn't claim to be the "savior of mankind" have not read, or do not accept, the straightforward claims of the Bible. Jesus repeatedly stated his identity and his mission. It is undeniably clear.

17

Ministry of Healing

Not long after Jesus returned to Cana where he turned water into wine, a prominent highly regarded citizen of Capernaum, twenty miles east, came looking for him. The man made his way through the exuberant crowd to get close enough to gain Jesus' attention. "My son is dying, and I need you to come right now," he pleaded. Jesus lamented that people only seemed to come around when they wanted something from him. "My son is dying!" the man restated in a panic. "You need to come now."

The man calmed down when Jesus looked him in the eye and assured him that his son was fine and he should go home. Half way to Capernaum he encountered his servants on their way to fetch him. "You're son is well," they excitedly told him. When he asked when his son started to recover they informed him it was one o'clock in the afternoon, precisely the time Jesus sent him on his way. The Bible indicates the man and his household became ardent followers. Given he was Peter's neighbor, it's likely they had encounters over the next couple of years. Jesus probably met the boy later and watched him grow. That the incident is documented is not surprising. The fact it spread through the community is highly likely.

Dozens of healing episodes are recorded in the New Testament. Jesus was credited with restoring sight to the blind, hearing to the deaf, and mobility to cripples. He banished illness and disease, put lunatics in their right mind, and helped derelicts and perverts overcome their bad habits and destructive practices. There was nothing Jesus was not able to overcome with the singular exception he never forced his healing spirit upon an unreceptive human will.

Physical people in a material world measure health by subjective carnal standards. Jesus referred to sighted people around him as blind. He said many of the people who heard him speak were deaf. He declared that physical health was secondary to mental health, and neither was of enduring consequence without spiritual health. "What good is it if you attain a fit body and a stable mind, if you allow your spirit to lapse into the abyss," he argued.

Before initiating miraculous healings Jesus often asked people if they believed, indicating they had to see God as unbound by the natural order he created. Jesus constantly drew distinction between the material universe and the spiritual realm we only experience by faith. On one occasion a man's epileptic son fell to the ground, thrashed about, banged his head on the floor, and kicked those who tried to help. The father's tearful appeal attracted Jesus, who approached and asked the man to put his faith in him. "I want to trust you, sir," the man replied. "Can you overlook my doubts?" That was enough for Jesus.

Upon Jesus' touch the boy became so limp those around supposed he died. When they helped him to his feet he was physically restored. Then Jesus drove home the point that he was not as concerned about people's physical condition as he was about their spirituality. Yet, Jesus clearly understood how difficult it is for people to focus on spiritual health when they're beset with physical problems.

Along the road from Galilee to Jerusalem Jesus encountered ten lepers. Those who were afflicted with leprosy were banished to leper colonies as soon as they were identified and diagnosed. It was a certain death knell. Ten hopeless lepers begged from a distance for help of any kind. Jesus approached to embrace and comfort those who craved his touch. When he reoriented them back under God's jurisdiction the malady was arrested and they were physically cured. The Bible doesn't state they grew new fingers or that their pocked and pitted skin became smooth, but the aggressive disease was arrested and organs and tissues were repaired as healthy cells began to replicate according to the DNA that produced and directed them. Over time, healthy cells displaced what was rotten, corrupt, or "evil".

The healed lepers ran to the Temple to be reinstated in society as prescribed by their law and customs. They were ecstatic to resume a semblance of normalcy. Only one came back to bow before Jesus and thank him. The others got their physical lives back, but Jesus said of the one who sought to recognize the source of his healing and returned to pay homage that he alone among them was "made whole".

As indicated from the opening chapters of the Bible, life is the manifestation of alignment with God. Jesus said, "I am the vine and you are branches. Apart from me you can do nothing. I get life from my father, the root source, and it flows through me into you to produce fruit." Severing the spirit of God from a living being is like snipping a stem from a vine. A rose stem in a vase can appear vibrant. It can feed its bud and make it flower. But it is doomed from the time it's clipped and its days are strictly numbered. As long as a healthy stem or branch is attached to a healthy vine or trunk that is rooted to its life generating source it is secure, and a severed dying branch can be grafted back into a healthy trunk enabling it to survive and even yield new fruit again.

People Jesus healed yearned for normality in the physical world. He taught that true life can't be measured on a physical scale. When he said he came to give "abundant life" he wasn't just addressing stronger limbs, improved vision, a better crop yield, or even extended time on Earth. The Bible states, "Jesus didn't cling to being exalted, but disregarded his personal reputation and took the form of a regular man, tempted and tested like every other man. Yet, unlike other men, he suffered and died rather than yielding to the natural inclination to sin."

At the garden in Eden sin was described as a state of being that arose out of separation from God's will and influence. Jesus, the Son of Man as he referred to himself, remained constantly calibrated to the will of God. The rightful heir of Adam's domain came to subdue and superintend the created material order. He did not dare turn off his spiritual receptors. That is why Christians consider Jesus to be both fully man and fully God. He was a physical being with an uncompromised spirit that was never impugned.

Such a state doesn't seem normal, or even attainable. Yet that's the rendering of the Bible from beginning to end, so it seems to be what was initially intended for people on Earth. The prophet Samuel said, "The Lord doesn't see as men see. Men look upon outward appearances, but God looks straight to the heart." People in the Bible were preoccupied with their physical circumstance. Jesus surmised their spiritual condition. We still are, and he still does.

18

What Jesus Taught

Jesus' lessons are sprinkled throughout the gospels of Matthew, Mark, Luke and John, and amplified in letters that were canonized into the New Testament. Matthew's training in the priesthood and tax recording suited him to document the actions of his mentor and friend, Jesus Christ, a Jew whose earliest followers came out of Judaism. Jesus fulfilled laws and expectations that were prescribed for the Jews. That needs to be understood to appreciate the Bible.

John Mark traveled with Barnabas and Paul, the first evangelical missionaries of the early church before becoming Peter's scribe and personal assistant. He wrote from Peter's perspective and recorded his stories. That's why the Gospel of Mark records so much about what happened to Peter.

Luke was a gentile who became a Christian without converting to Judaism. He was a medical doctor and a scholar. After meeting Paul, the missionary apostle, he became obsessed with chronicling Jesus' life. He met various original disciples, studied with Jews, and traveled with missionaries. He interviewed Jesus' mother and captured many of her early memories. Matthew recorded Jesus' Davidic ancestry through Joseph to Solomon, but Luke recorded Jesus' ancestry through Mary's father Eli to Nathan.

Jesus recruited John while he was mending his father's fishing nets. That was prophetic. Matthew, Mark and Luke wrote synoptic gospels. Years later, John tied their stories together as if stitching a net. Every epistle in the New Testament had been written when John penned 1st, 2nd, and 3rd John, synching up everyone else's instructions and warnings and validated them from a credible original source. He wrapped up the entire Bible at the end of the first century by writing his revelation of end-time events.

The fullest account of Jesus' teaching was preserved by Matthew in a segment of scripture we refer to as his sermon on the mount. All of Jesus' sayings were recreated based on memories recorded ten to twenty years after the actual events. It should be noted and accepted that Jesus' talmidim shared the same stories for decades, and every one of them died a martyrs' death rather than recant.

John stated that if he composed all the firsthand accounts he personally witnessed there wouldn't be enough books to contain them. The firsthand documentation at their disposal was more than the apostles could convey, but they left a viable and useful record that has stood the test of time. Many have tried to discredit it and ended up becoming major proponents of Jesus' movement.

Jesus' sermon began with eight beatitudes, or sources of paradoxical good fortune. "Blessed are those who have exhausted their own resources and come up lacking; the spiritual domain is finally within reach. Blessed are those who harbor remorse and regret; they will be comforted. Blessed are those who get broken and submit to God; in the end, they'll acquire what's best for them. Blessed are those who yearn for justice to prevail; ultimately they will be satisfied.

"Blessed are those who tolerate others; God will be lenient with them. Blessed are those who humbly open up to God; God will reveal himself to them. Blessed are those who reconcile other people to God; they will be adopted into God's family. And blessed are those who are put down for an unwavering commitment to righteousness; they will inherit an elevated station with God."

Jesus said, "You are salt on the Earth, here to flavor and preserve, but if salt loses its saline capacity it gets discarded. You're like a city on a hillside, lit up on a dark night to guide wayward drifters home. Don't let anything extinguish the light." Then he laid out a new higher standard than the law demanded. "You were taught that murder is killing another person. But I say it would be better to kill their mortal body than to destroy their fragile spirit. Whoever initiates a verbal assault should be scolded. Whoever intimidates or abuses a vulnerable soul should be harshly reprimanded. But whoever destroys another person's sense of personal worth should burn in hell. If you come to realize you've hurt someone, go make amends before you approach God in worship. Otherwise, you might be surprised when you are confronted by the testimony against you. You could be arrested, tried and convicted in the court of Heaven. You can't afford the penalty that will be meted out against you for such an offense.

"You've been warned about adultery. I say mental transgressions are equal to physical violations. Don't lapse into a compromising situation. Be careful what you pledge. Let your yes mean yes, and your no mean no. Make every effort to live up to your promises and fulfill your vows and obligations.

"Revenge is sweet, but I say let it go. Hold on to your principles, yet don't get lured into a fight and don't harbor a grudge. Be a giver and rise above those who aggravate you. Everybody tolerates a friend, but I admonish you to extend an open hand to your adversaries as well. Raise your aspirations to reflect godly character, but don't make a spectacle of yourself or flaunt your spirituality. That's counterproductive. Keep your piety between you and God. If you draw others to laud your goodness that's all the recompense you'll get. Humbly focus on whether God is privately pleased with you. No one can serve two masters. You'll either serve one and neglect the other, or obey one and ignore the other. Choose whether you're striving for a material or a spiritual blessing.

"It's not your place to judge others or direct the world, that's God's job. Generally, people don't set themselves up for success. They meander through life without acknowledging life's objective. Establish a routine of following God and pursuing his aims. The path of life is straight and narrow and demands a sense of discipline. The road to ruin is comfortable and convenient, but it's easy to wander off course."

Jesus said those who listened to and followed him were like people who built their lives on a solid foundation. They would be able to withstand the storms of life. People who didn't pay attention or neglected to follow his advice were building an insecure structure on an unstable foundation that would crumble under adversity. Like prophets of old, Jesus didn't give advice he couldn't reconcile with scriptural principles. Jesus taught people how to please God by following the Bible's prescribed ordinances. He taught that motives and intent were as important as deeds and outcome. Jesus was a credible authoritative source who personally modeled everything he said and taught.

19

Miracles, Signs, and Wonders

The greatest hurdle people face in accepting the Bible rests in the supernatural events presented in both the Old and New Testaments. We can allow for what we cannot know if we can hold the hope of gaining insight through future discovery. The Bethlehem Star illustrates that premise. And the fact that archeological expeditions have uncovered so much evidence in support of the Bible's previously unfounded claims helps us get beyond other hurdles we encounter.

As long as we can latch onto a reasonable explanation we can accept almost anything. The rift comes when occurrences appear absolutely indefensible. No one knows how the world began so anyone can speculate to the degree his imagination will allow. Viable assumptions based on prior knowledge and established principles generate substance for a valid foundation, even if it's subject to change.

The fact a normal cell becomes cancerous automatically allows for a cancer cell to be made normal. That the human body heals itself in accordance with the DNA contained in every cell that is not anatomically damaged or suppressed is now medically and scientifically accepted. With age the process breaks down for a reason not yet discovered. Since we now know we could clone an entire eye from a single healthy eye cell, we can begin to fathom the miraculous healing of blind people.

But we are stretched when otherwise marginally acceptable events defy the limits of time and space. We can allow for a blind man being healed, but instantly? By atomic fusion we could imagine the conversion of water to wine, but in six small open barrels? As stated in the beginning of this book, the Bible does not argue for acceptance, it assumes faith. "Faith is the substance of things hoped for; the evidence of things unseen."

If there is a force beyond our material existence how can we know how that force relates to our physical universe? And by what means could such a force intervene, and how would that be manifested? A man who invents a clock can enter it and make changes at will. So why couldn't a God who made the universe similarly impose his will? How could we be expected to understand how it happened or what he was doing?

And if someone tapped into that source could he not be used as a medium for change? If everything that is physical is rooted in a spiritual source that changes our understanding of everything. It is one thing to have access to laser technology, it is something else to understand it and know how to apply it. It's one thing to use a laser. It is quite another to be one. Jesus said, "I am the vine, and you are branches." He also said, "I and my Father are one (in the same)." The Bible becomes a different book when you can adopt that perspective.

Two gospel writers recorded Jesus supernaturally multiplying food to feed a hungry multitude that gathered in the plains of Galilee. In John's account the crowd was estimated at five thousand men plus women and children. Let's say there were twelve thousand people present. Many of them had likely followed Jesus for a while. "Where can we get enough to feed so many?" Jesus asked his disciples, knowing full well what he had in mind.

Andrew found a young lad with a picnic basket he was willing to share. It had five loaves of barley bread and two small fish in it. It was probably intended for his family. What local market do you know of where you could pick up enough groceries to feed twelve thousand people on the spur of the moment? It would take at least 3,000 pounds of fish, cleaned, filleted and cooked, to give everyone a small portion. Then you would need 4,000 small loaves of bread torn into thirds to give everyone just one serving.

In today's currency you would spend over eighty thousand dollars sending that crowd through a local drive through restaurant. If you issued one serving every ten seconds it would take over thirty three hours to get everyone a first helping and the Bible says everyone ate as much as they wanted. Then, when everyone had eaten, Jesus' apprentices gathered over twelve baskets of leftovers.

The narrative reveals that Jesus first separated those present into 240 groups of fifty. That means each of twelve apprentices oversaw twenty groups. It's likely that several families packed a lunch for the occasion and when Jesus offered his prayer over the food, as recorded, those who had food shared with those who lacked. It's probable that those present didn't have a huge craving in the midst of the activities that afternoon. Jesus wasn't inclined to eat when his disciples brought him food at Jacob's well in Sychar. We've all foregone our appetite in the midst of festivities.

Organized into groups who shared what they had and ate simultaneously, it would have taken less than two hours to eat, clean up, collect the leftovers and bring them to Jesus. But it's also possible that a spiritual force intervened in the physical world and circumvented or accelerated the natural order to produce an otherwise unexplainable outcome. The degree to which a person struggles to accept this and similar occurrences recorded in the Bible is probably a good measure of that person's capacity to trust God and yield his allegiance to an unseen sovereign entity. But either scenario works.

As stated at the onset of this book, the Bible is not a history book or a science text. It's a chronicle of every man's spiritual pilgrimage in a material world. To the extent you can absorb and process, or chew and digest, what you read, you can grow to understand a spiritual force engaged in your own life. Jesus asked his men what they had and he knew it wasn't enough. Jesus had no problem stepping out with the full assurance that God was able and willing to provide for every need according to his own limitless resources, good intentions, and perfect understanding. That's the life Jesus modeled.

20

Aggravating Religious Leaders

Clerics from Jerusalem travelled to Capernaum to confront Jesus concerning what he was alleged to have said and done. The house was crowded and onlookers outside made it inaccessible. Four young men transported a crippled friend on his bed mat. They couldn't get to the door so they scaled a wall and got on the roof where they dismantled a section and hoisted him down in front of the assembled dignitaries. Acknowledging the faith that drove their pursuit, Jesus told the invalid, "Be glad young man, the sin that severed you from God has been resolved. Gather your belongings and go home." The fellow made it to his feet, collected his bedding, and walked out the door to the cheers of the crowd.

The elite priests took offense. "Who are you to forgive sins?" they demanded with indignation.

Jesus replied, "Would you prefer that I just say he's healed instead of pointing out that his physical health has been restored because he's been reconnected to his spiritual source?" They considered that the young man was paying for sins he committed. Jesus dealt with sin in relation to the young man's disposition toward God. Religious elitists look at fairness in regard to penalty. Jesus showed that making things right is better than punishing. He often said mercy is preferable to sacrifice. They were so legalistic they had a hard time accepting his logic. Religion doesn't always equate with righteousness.

Later, when Jesus visited Jerusalem for a holiday, clerics stormed toward him holding a woman who was screaming and crying. Her husband caught her with another man and brought her to the Temple. Adultery was a capital offense punishable by stoning, and the judges found her guilty. Seventy priests composed the Sanhedrin, which was tantamount to a Supreme Court. Very seldom did seventy clerics hear the same case. It took only two of three to resolve a civil dispute. Twelve had to agree in a capital case, and they needed at least a two vote margin to secure a guilty verdict.

The priests had a dilemma. They found the woman guilty of a capital crime, but couldn't execute her without Roman approval. Historians have indicated that when the Sanhedrin engaged in stoning a Jew, which they still did on occasion, Roman overseers looked the other way. The priests wanted to put Jesus on the spot. They knew his background and it appears they intended to entrap him. "This woman was caught in the very act of adultery," they began. "You've presented yourself as a legal expert by traveling around teaching people how to follow our laws. What do you propose we do to her?" An anxious crowd gathered round as Jesus knelt and wrote something in the dirt with his finger. They pressed him again.

Jesus stood to publicly confront the issue and proposed that whoever didn't bear sin of his own should step forward and have the honor of throwing the first stone. One by one, from the most prominent to the least of them, they dropped their rocks and retreated to their sanctuary. "Who stands to accuse you?" he asked the woman. When she looked around and saw no one, he said, "Nor do I condemn you. Now go. And don't ever stray from God again." The Bible does not follow her, but it seems clear she was genuinely repentant. The law was written in stone. Jesus may have etched the woman's crime in the dust where he could wipe it out to be observed no more. Yet Jesus understood, better than the priests, that every transgression of the law has a price.

Jesus often turned the tables on Temple priests. They set traps for him and he publicly humiliated them time and again. Since they couldn't trip him up, they staged a trap in order to provoke the Romans to arrest him for treason. In a public square with Roman officials looking on they asked a trick question. "The Torah mitzvot state that we're to use our resources to support the Temple, take care of our needy, and build our own nation. Isn't it a violation of our law for us to pay tribute to a foreign government?"

Jesus asked for a coin and someone handed him a Roman denarius, the currency of the day. "Whose image is stamped on this object?" he asked, holding it up. When they acknowledged that Caesar's image was imprinted on the coin he clutched it and looked into their faces. "Then give Caesar what is rightfully his according to what he has provided. And give God back what is cast in his image." The humiliated priests slipped away and a great crowd of peasants gathered to hear more.

When he healed a beggar who was born blind, multitudes were drawn to pursue Jesus as their savior. After confirming that the beggar was willing to fully trust him, Jesus scooped up dirt and spit in it to make a mud patch that he placed directly on the man's open eyeballs. Jesus observed that God used the elements of Earth to create a perfect man, and acknowledged that healing broken spirits on Earth is uncomfortable and sometimes painful. Jesus directed the man to wash the dirt out of his eyes in the pool of Siloam and when he did what Jesus told him to do, he saw clearly for the first time. Many people had seen the man begging at the fountain at the Watergate entrance to the city and knew who he was. The episode further elevated Jesus' stature among both the common masses and the ruling elite.

The priests sent guards to seize the healed man who caused a stir so they could publicly interrogate him. They brought his parents in to confirm that he was, in fact, blind from his birth. When the clerics demanded that the poor dirty beggar in tattered clothes renounce Jesus, he embarrassed them far worse than they had previously experienced. "Earlier today I didn't know who this man, Jesus, was, and couldn't have cared less," he stated. "But no one has ever healed a person who was born blind. He gave me sight and I can only conclude he's empowered by God. How can I renounce what I have actually personally experienced? If you can't see the truth that's right in front of you, maybe you need to call Jesus in here to fix your eyes too." When the laughter subsided the chief priests started plotting in earnest to get rid of Jesus. They put a bounty of thirty pieces of silver on him and hired assassins to bring him in, dead or alive.

Jesus found out what they were up to and retreated back to Galilee where he and his men lived in caves in the mountains of Ephraim for several months. Jesus knew who he was and what he was capable of, but he exercised wisdom and restraint. He didn't take matters into his own hands, but sought to do only what God inspired him to do when God nudged him to do it. Jesus' fate was sealed and Luke records in his gospel that, "Jesus steadfastly set his face toward Jerusalem." That means throughout the rest of his time among men, Jesus was singularly focused on what lay in store for him in Jerusalem.

21

Raising Lazarus

A few close friends knew where Jesus was staying in the hills of Ephraim in Galilee. When Jesus came to Judea for holiday feasts he often stayed with Lazarus and his sisters in Bethany a few miles east of Jerusalem. Mary and Martha sent word that their brother was deathly ill and asked Jesus to come quickly. Jesus told the messengers the illness would not end Lazarus' life, but that it had come upon him so God might be glorified. He sent them home and lingered in Galilee. The band knew that the heads of state put a price on Jesus' head and it wasn't safe for him to travel in the vicinity of the capital.

Days later, Jesus approached his men and told them Lazarus was "komata", from which we derive comatose, and he needed to go pay him a visit. They figured if Lazarus was resting and they were safe in Galilee, they should stay put. Then Jesus explained that Lazarus died, and he was compelled to go. Believing they would be walking into a certain death trap they unanimously resisted until Thomas, whom Jesus referred to as didymus, broke rank. Thomas reminded them of their mutual pledge and convinced the others they had no choice but to go where Jesus took them, even if it meant they had to die with him.

By the time they arrived, Lazarus had been dead for four days. When Martha heard that Jesus was approaching, she left the mourners and ran to meet him. "If you had only come when we begged you, our brother wouldn't have had to die," she sobbed. "I know God would grant whatever you asked for."

When Jesus told her that her brother was going to arise again, she at first assumed he was talking about the afterlife. "I can resurrect him. I am the source of life," he boldly proclaimed. "Anyone who puts his faith in me while he lives will never really die. He won't be bound by mortal death. Do you believe me? Do you understand?"

"Yes, Lord," she replied, no longer crying. "I believe you are the Christ, the son of God and savior of men." Then she went home and told her sister that she too needed to come to Jesus. All of the house guests went out with Mary and Martha to meet Jesus in a public park.

Mary fell at Jesus' feet and wept, "Oh, my Lord, where have you been? If you had only showed up when we summoned you, our brother would be alive."

Seeing how they mourned, Jesus asked his friends to take him to the tomb where they laid the body. When tears welled up in his eyes those around perceived Jesus loved his dear friend and wondered why he hadn't come to his aid while he still might have spared him from dying. "Roll the access stone away," Jesus uttered to their amazement. Martha reminded him Lazarus had been dead for several days and his body was decomposing. The stench of death emanated from the grave. "Did I not tell you that if you put your trust in me you would behold the awesome glory of God?" he confidently replied. As his apprentices rolled the tombstone away, Jesus lifted his gaze and began to pray.

"Father, I thank you for hearing me. I realize you monitor my every thought, but for the sake of those gathered here I verbalize my intentions so they might know for certain that you sent me." Then he turned his focus to the cave tomb and bellowed, "Come to me, Lazarus!"

When a form wrapped in linen with his face still hidden behind a burial cloth appeared at the entrance of the tomb Jesus ordered his apprentices to unbind him and set him free. Someone from the crowd excitedly ran to the Temple to let the priests know what happened. Those in attendance were overwhelmed and never questioned Jesus' authority again. But when the callous religious leaders came out to verify it, many of them concluded it was some kind of trick. Because it violated nature and logic, they refused to accept it.

We live in an ordered world of space, time, matter and energy. Our experiences, and the influence of those we trust, lead us to determine what we accept as real. There are many things that are real that we cannot explain. Earlier, when someone asked Jesus to prove he was Christ, he replied, "Even if someone came back from the dead, you wouldn't believe him." On another occasion Jesus told the Pharisees that the only credential he would provide would be related to Jonah's time in the belly of a sea creature.

Jesus commanded faith. The Bible says, "Without faith it is impossible to please God. He rewards those who diligently seek him." The opposite of faith is not doubt as one might assume. Doubt is actually a form of negative faith that something may not be real, or might not happen. The opposite of faith is knowledge. If someone predisposes that something is true, faith is not required or applied.

There's a subtle difference between assumed knowledge and absolute faith. Assumed knowledge is intellectual closure. Absolute faith is spiritual openness. A true scientist exercises both. He is open to discovery based on new exposure and experience. A pseudo scientist seeks to prove or reinforce a predetermined hypothesis. No one can comprehend the essence of Christ without applying both faith and reason.

We know life emanates from a force beyond the realm of the physical universe. Yet men try in vain to make it conform to their preconceptions. Those who have difficulty with the Bible are not more intellectual, on the contrary they are simply more vested in the notion that someday someone will find material answers for mysteries that are perceived as spiritual in nature.

The clerics of the Sanhedrin refused to accept that a man once blind could see, a man once crippled could walk, or a man once dead could breathe. They did not lack intelligence. Like the rich young ruler who could not let go of his fortune in order to accept what Jesus offered, they were simply too vested in their secular worldview. As stated in the early chapters of this book, men haven't changed much. Jesus gave sight to the blind, but he could not make people see the spiritual domain through physical eyes. "Having eyes, you see not. Having ears, you hear not," he often lamented.

Part 3

The Christ's Mission

22

Confronting the Establishment

When Jesus returned to Jerusalem to celebrate the Passover Feast in April of 33AD he knew it would be his last trip. He spent the last six months of his life preparing his closest disciples to carry on after he was gone. His lessons were more intense and somber. There was more urgency in his lectures. He openly discussed his impending crucifixion, though much of what he said flew over his listeners' heads as they later admitted in their writings.

Jewish historians have estimated there were well over a million people in and around Jerusalem for the holiday. Jesus and his twelve apprentices most likely arrived in Bethany three miles east of Jerusalem on Friday, the 7th of Nisan in the year 3793 on the Jewish lunar calendar. They stayed at the home of Simon the leper, whom Jesus had healed at the onset of his public ministry. Scholars have advanced that Simon may have been Judas Iscariot's father. That would give Hebrew cultural credence to the arrangement.

Those who didn't have a relative or close friend to stay with camped in public areas, pastures, or orchards like the one on the hillside between

Bethany and Jerusalem that was popularly known as Gethsemane Garden on the western slope of the Mount of Olives just across the Kidron Valley. It's likely that hundreds of families slept there every night during the weeklong festival.

The evening of their arrival ushered in a Sabbath, or what we call Saturday. Hebrews reckoned days from sunset to sunset. Darkness preceded light so each day ended and began when light had run its course and a new darkness set in. There were four watches through the night designated by the position of starry constellations easily observed overhead. The day was divided into twelve hours that were determined by the Sun's position in the sky.

The Sun rose in the first hour and peaked at noon, which was known as the sixth hour. The third hour would correspond to nine o'clock in the morning. The eleventh hour was the last hour for work. People wrapped up what they were doing and put things away in the twelfth hour so they could be home in bed before it got dark. Any part of a day counted as a day so technically 9PM Tuesday to 6PM Wednesday our time would have been one day, but 6PM Wednesday to 9PM Wednesday would have been considered two days. In summer, days were longer, so hours were longer and night watches grew correspondingly shorter.

The month of Nisan, called Abib in biblical times, marked the equinox. From the full moon of Passover, daytime grew progressively longer than nighttime in Earth's northern hemisphere. Jews said that "light conquered darkness." Springtime ushered in new growth and another harvest season. Earth was "reborn". Moses established that Passover should be observed on the fourteenth day of the first month each year in remembrance of the death angel passing over homes of those who displayed the blood of a lamb on their doorposts and lentils as God miraculously saved Israel from bondage in a land where they were aliens. The 14th day is the exact middle of a lunar month and the moon would be full and bright on that next Friday. It almost never rained in Israel in late March and early April.

The Sabbath was a day of worship and rest. On Saturday, the 8th, Jesus went to the Temple and was greeted with a robust reception, notwithstanding there was still a bounty of a full month's wages for his apprehension. His confident public discourse and open defiance put the establishment priests on their heels. A confrontation could trigger a full scale rebellion. Common people clearly sided with Jesus over their corrupt oppressive government leaders. The Romans and the Jews were on edge.

On Sunday morning the stage was set. Jesus rode into Jerusalem through the only gate that lead directly to the Temple grounds on the back of a mule colt, the offspring of a horse and a donkey bred to carry a heavy load. It had been more than three decades since Jesus' mother rode a donkey into Bethlehem near the time the soon to be Caesar Tiberius rode a stallion through the gates of Rome in a victory parade after his conquests in Europe. Flanked by his talmidim, hundreds of enthusiastic supporters welcomed Jesus into the capital city for what many assumed would be the coronation of a new Jewish king who would repel the Romans, clean up the Temple, and lead Israel to her former glory. That was their idea, but that's not what Jesus had in mind.

The leaders couldn't ignore Jesus' swelling popularity, but every time they confronted him he got the better of them. Caiaphas, the Head Priest, personally addressed Jesus and demanded he tell people to stop cheering for him. Jesus replied, "If you squelch the innocent voices of the masses, nature itself will cry out. Truth and nature must run their course. No one can suppress either indefinitely. Nor can whatever is without merit be sustained." Truth will always survive and eventually surface. Jesus stated that he was the essence of every man's reality. His "I am", the core of his being, was truth. He did not twist, hide from, or avoid it.

Caiaphas and his secular peers who governed the land refused to submit because they refused to see. Like pseudo scientists, they had to cling to their established worldview or give up everything that gave meaning to their vain lives. They would not see from Jesus' perspective, though Jesus could see from theirs and tried to warn them. Jesus ached for them but would not impose his will. The Bible declares that, "Every man is right in his own eyes," and every man is individually accountable before God.

Jesus was so in tune with God and so well versed in the holy scriptures that everything he did over the next week confirmed, complied with, and fulfilled what had been mysteriously recorded by dozens of writers over several centuries. What they composed was finally exposed. That which had been concealed was at last revealed. What the Torah contained could now be explained. Daily, Jesus lived out obscure prophecies.

Suffice to say that all of history, the essence of mankind's existence on Earth, is bound up in this simple story imparted to us through those to whom God entrusted it. It's so complex that the greatest scholar in the world could not fully digest it in an extended lifetime of study. And it is so simple that an innocent little child could take a bite and be fully satisfied.

23

A Last Supper Together

Some say Jesus Christ was anti-authoritarian, anti-establishment, or divisive. They are mistaken. Jesus Christ remains confrontational to this day, but he was never disruptive of the natural order or a legitimate civil structure. He righteously advocated for and followed the rule of law to the letter. He did not call for rebellion. In fact, he commanded absolute allegiance to God at all cost. In so doing he warned that would create conflict with those who opposed God or advocated for a contending master. He promoted allegiance to the Temple, telling people to follow the teachings of the priests without following their hypocritical example. He adhered to traditional family structure, maintained relational purity and always considered others' long term best interests above his immediate satisfaction.

Two recorded events have been put forward to advance the notion that Jesus was not fully submissive to his parents. In the first case, he was left behind at the Temple at the age of twelve. The other instance occurred at a wedding party in Cana where his mother observed the host was running out of wine. In both instances some translations don't capture the original language and culture. "Did you not consider that I would be pursuing my father's interests?" was a respectful and humble reply; as was "Madam, what has that got to do with me?" In both cases, the Bible text follows Jesus responses with a commendation of his subsequent immediate behavior. Jesus adhered to and promoted the natural family order and criticized those who deviated from it. The purity and commitment he spoke of and exemplified dissolve any claim of impropriety on his part, otherwise he absolutely discredited himself.

Jesus was also a good Jew. He not only studied, analyzed, and memorized the Torah, he became the Torah. He nibbled, bit, chewed, swallowed, and digested it. It was the fiber of his being. What came out of him was Torah. He was a human whose physical being had fully absorbed a spiritual essence. He was no longer calibrated to carnal desires or worldly aspirations, but to the will of God. Jesus was inspired to act and react in accordance to his spiritual orientation.

Jesus never intended to obliterate the Temple, but to purge it. When it couldn't be purged, he circumvented it. That was the plan developed from the onset. Only as events unfolded could we see how perfectly they lay upon their predisposed template. Jesus could detect the convergence of history and prophecy. He foresaw the end of his earthly journey. Like a rafter riding rapids in a rushing river he didn't have to forge ahead, only navigate through each turbulent moment and every dangerous turn.

Whole books are dedicated to the observance of the Passover from Jewish and Christian perspectives. The symbolic significance of the various elements of preparation and the meal itself cannot be addressed in a single chapter. Deeper insight requires further study, and would be rewarding. But several points make Jesus' last supper unique. It was a prophetic pinnacle. On Sunday, by law, the head of every household in Israel selected or procured a paschal lamb. It was to be a male from among the flock. It was to be young, strong, and without scars, blemishes or injury. It was a sin offering to God so the better the specimen the more effective the sacrifice. On Sunday people who came to shop for a lamb were drawn to Jesus as he rode into the city.

Over the next several days the lamb was to be isolated and inspected. It was tested to assure viability. Over the same span Jesus stood before the priests and scribes. He preached to the masses. They watched him, and drilled him, and challenged him, and found him to be without equal. He was physically, mentally, emotionally and spiritually sound and perfectly healthy.

On Thursday bread was quickly prepared and put in the oven without yeast or leaven in order to accelerate baking. Yeast represented sin. Bread was a combination of flour ground from earthen grain, pure water provided from above, and a pinch of salt. Because there was no yeast, the bread didn't rise and get puffed up. That was a picture of humility. The flat bread, called matzah, was beaten, punctured, pressed, scratched and scored into three parts. Then it was placed in a hot oven and set aside for a great supper to honor the time when God reclaimed his people. The men of the household grabbed and subdued their chosen lamb. They laid their hands on it, prayed over it, slaughtered it, and hung it out to purge its blood. Then it was skewered to become the central attraction and main course at a feast celebrating Israel's deliverance.

Jesus could have stayed at Simon's house as a guest, but chose to oversee his own Passover with his apprentices as master of ceremonies in a borrowed elevated room. Moses' law commanded all Jews to stand while eating in honor of the original Passover in Egypt. Then, as in medieval times, slaves stood to eat. Family members and guest were at other times normally seated at a table. Royalty, of course, reclined to eat. When the apprentices entered the upper room to enjoy the banquet Jesus prepared for them they were stunned to see food on a platform four to eight inches above the ground with cushions around it. This was their graduation ceremony. "Previously, I called you students and subordinates," Jesus began. "Tonight you are my friends." He then opened up to reveal his most intimate thoughts and encouraged them to practice what he taught and carry on what he had invested in them. That night, while the nation of Israel ate like slaves, Jesus and his first close followers dined like royalty.

There are fourteen stages of the Passover Seder. There's hidden meaning behind each aspect of the formally regimented meal, explained in song by the patriarch or master of ceremonies through the course of the evening. The ninth step is called Maror after the bitter leaves or stalks that are dipped into charoset. Today, Jews dip celery or broccoli into horseradish then a sweet mixture of cinnamon, nuts, apples, and pears in a sweet red wine. The stinging effect of the raw horseradish that draws tears is countered by the sweet blend that softens the blow but doesn't prevent it. It leaves a bitter aftertaste to remind ancestral Jews of the travails and struggles of bondage. When someone at the table had a special burden, another could dip for them to "share their maror". It was like saying, "I feel your pain." This gracious gesture, when applied, was intended to provide comfort, reassurance, or even forgiveness.

"This is the last meal I will share with you until we feast together in the kingdom where my father reigns," Jesus told his disciples. "You expect me to rise up and lead," he acknowledged. "You want to be elevated with me." Then he turned their world upside down saying, "True greatness is not measured in ruling but serving." And Jesus modeled his message by washing their dirty feet.

"You've observed what I've done," Jesus said. "Now I extend to you the same offer God afforded me. The one regarded as most prominent among you will be the one who's most humble and least self-centered. I didn't come here to be a slave master, but a guide. I've come to teach, encourage, and empower fellow slaves. I've come to set people free and help them live and grow. Please join me." Those who look forward to "reigning" with Christ might be surprised when they're directed to turn in any crowns and put on an apron.

When they finished their meal, the entourage left the rented chamber and passed through the festive streets of Jerusalem. The Bible says they sang hymns and Jesus continued teaching along the way. Surely thousands of people poured out of Jerusalem with them, singing and dancing. There wouldn't have been room for those who hosted the dinners to put all their guests up for the night, so they returned to their encampments and settled down.

24

Arrest in a Garden

Friday, Nisan 14th, a bright full moon lit the streets of Jerusalem and paths in nearby orchards like a lantern. Upon finishing their Passover meal Jesus and his men walked among reveling Jews on their way to camp out in Gethsemane Garden across the Kidron Valley. They must have stayed there often because the gospel writers recorded this was one of Jesus' favorite familiar spots.

Judas Iscariot departed the banquet early but knew exactly where he could find his boss. In the third watch of the night, which was just after midnight, he would make his way across the stream at the bottom of the valley with a gang of Temple Guards and clerics. Several cups of wine were served as part of the Passover feast and the partying continued into the night. The voices of men singing traditional Passover songs and psalms could be heard for miles. This was a major celebration and many less disciplined Jews became intoxicated. Secular Jews, and there were many, used the occasion as an excuse to drink to excess. The path was lined with rowdy people. Campers who settled down were kept awake late into the night.

Looking out over Jerusalem, still lit with torches and candles, with men dancing in the streets and on the Temple grounds, Jesus curiously stated, "You're in for a rough night. Like the scroll says, 'When the shepherd is smitten, the sheep will scatter.' But I'll meet up with you after I've been restored. It's time for my identity to be disclosed and my father's plan to be revealed." The disciples were speechless. They had no idea what he was talking about.

Jesus told his friends to get some rest while he went deeper into the garden to pray in solitude. He asked Peter, James and John to stand watch, as though he might be expecting an intrusion. He was disappointed when they fell asleep instead of standing guard. Jesus knew they were exhausted from the long day of holiday mirth, and they each drank at least four cups of wine. However, Jesus justly expected his followers to match his devotion to them.

As he agonized in prayer, the Bible states that drops of blood mingled with sweat dripped from his face. The intensity of his meditation brought on a condition medically referred to as hematohidrosis. It would probably have been alien to those who witnessed it at the time. Jesus must have foreseen what was coming because the Bible says he pleaded with God to let it pass. He did not want to drink the cup before him. "Nevertheless, not my will, but thine be done," he concluded.

Having resolved the issue, Jesus was ready to face whatever came his way. From now on there would be no more deciding; no choosing. All he had to do was comply. Some scholars say Jesus could still have avoided his fate. The Bible reveals the matter was resolved in the garden, not in the court or on the cross. From that point on, Jesus simply accepted what befell him, having placed himself completely at God's disposal to do, and to be used for, whatever God had in store.

Jesus assured the success of his mission by fully acquiescing to God without reservation or recourse and by modeling everything he taught about spiritual guidance in a material world. What was determined at the beginning of time and resolved in a garden, now needed only to be enacted to completion.

Observing men with torches and swords crossing the bridge to make their way into the orchard that surrounded Gethsemane Garden, Jesus alerted his men, "Wake up. The time has come for me to be put to the test." Immediately, they got up and surrounded him. Knowing precisely why the ravenous pack approached, Jesus stepped forward as they arrived. "Who are you looking for?" he confidently asked. Upon hearing his voice, the mob stopped abruptly, stumbling and falling at his feet. Judas stepped up and greeted him with a kiss and called him "Boss", identifying him to the others. "How can you betray me with such warm pleasantries?" Jesus grinned. "My friend, you've been deceived."

Judas' countenance fell.

"Are you Jesus of Nazareth?" a guard inquired.

"I am," came the simple reply. "What do you want with me?"

The guard fumbled and asked again, "Are you Jesus of Nazareth?"

"I am," Jesus restated. "If it's me you seek, let everyone else go."

The mob rushed to grab him. The disciples intervened and resisted. Peter drew his large fishing knife and slashed the ear of the High Priest's chief administrator. Jesus quieted the crowd and told Peter to put away his weapon. "Those who initiate violence subject themselves to violence," he declared. "Do you not realize that upon my request, Father would dispatch legions of angels to insulate and defend me? But then, how would what has been written beforehand be fulfilled? I'm fully confident God has posted his angels all around me."

Then he turned again to the mob. "Why approach me like I'm a violent adversary?" He reached out and restored Malchius' ear. "You didn't latch onto me when I taught openly at the Temple in broad daylight. But then, it's more your style to operate in darkness."

At that, they seized him. And in accordance with his prediction, his friends fled. The mob bound and blindfolded him. They beat, kicked, and spat on him. They mocked him and prodded him to tell them who hit him, and prophesy who was going to hit him next.

They didn't reenter Jerusalem through the main gate where Roman soldiers stood watch, but found a breach in the wall near the Dung Gate that led to the perpetually burning trash heap in the valley of the Sons of Hinnom, known as Gehenna, that stretched along the southern edge of the city. Once inside the city, they followed a route which took them to the home of Annas, the High Priest's father-in-law, who still pulled the cords of power in the Sanhedrin.

25

Mock Trial

Caiaphas summoned at least a dozen likeminded clerics. He chose a jury he could influence and control. They scripted a mockery of a trial, predetermined a verdict, and assigned witnesses to bear false testimony. There was still some reveling, but by now the city had quieted down. Celebrants were sleeping and would rise later than usual, many with a headache. A noisy crowd passing through the streets would not invite suspicion at two or three o'clock in the morning. Guards coming out to a garden in an olive orchard to make an arrest wouldn't have seemed out of line. Few people would have given much thought to a pilgrim's arrest, especially after a scuffle with Temple guards.

When Caiaphas was ready, he summoned Jesus from his father-in-law's house. The mob scaled a narrow stairway that was carved into a stone hillside and exists today as a tourist attraction. They entered a thirty by fifty foot stone patio overlooking Mount Zion and the City of David with the Temple as a backdrop. It was cool, so fires were kindled in pits at the corners of the patio and adjacent to the house.

While Caiaphas, Annas, and a few high ranking priests finalized their plans for the drama that unfolded, Jesus waited outside and prepared for another round of being mocked and beaten. Again, neighbors would not have thought the commotion unusual coming from a gathering at the High Priest's mansion. Peter and John dared to enter the patio and mingle with the restless crowd. Peter made eye-contact with Jesus as a rooster crowed. It was dawn of Friday. Peter fled. John stayed and quietly observed.

Caiaphas approached Jesus as if inspecting a statue. He inquired about his doctrine and asked what kind of mischief he was stirring up with his teaching. "I've been very open in public," Jesus responded. "You know very well what I've said, and what I believe."

A Temple guard standing alongside launched a backhand to Jesus' blood-caked bearded face. Jesus stumbled backward, but kept his balance. His hands were bound. "Show some respect, fool!" screamed the guard. "You'd better start giving your priests the answers they're looking for."

"Show me where I'm wrong," Jesus replied resolutely. "Or is it protocol now to slap people for speaking truth in a court of law in Israel?" Jesus had nothing more to say as Caiaphas and the others prodded him mercilessly. They brought in witnesses, but failed to generate a compelling case. At last, Caiaphas pleaded with Jesus to tell them clearly whether he was the Messiah, or Christ, the Son of God and savior of the world. "I am," he stated emphatically. "It really doesn't matter if you believe me or not. Eventually you're going to look up and see Adam's heir sitting at the right hand of God."

Caiaphas ripped his clothes and bellowed, "You heard it from his own mouth. This trial is adjourned. He just confessed to blasphemy, a capital offense." The crowd rushed him, screaming, punching, kicking, and spitting on him. Gleefully, they stood him up, bound his arms to his sides, and marched him off to Pontius Pilate, the Roman governor of the region.

John followed as the mob shoved Jesus through now empty streets, poking him with sticks. Most citizens were sleeping. When they reached the Governor's quarters, soldiers recognized the Head Priest and invited him in. Caiaphas explained that it was a holy day and entering pagan grounds would defile him so he couldn't administer the upcoming holiday rituals. Pilate had to come out.

On this particular year Passover preparation began on Thursday. As the sun set on Friday everyone ate the Passover meal by candlelight. The Feast of Unleavened Bread commenced Saturday, the day after Passover, which happened to be a Sabbath. Sunday marked the Feast of First Fruits. Saturday would be an important High Holy Sabbath and Caiaphas wanted to preside. The next three days presented an eerily unusual sacred phenomenon on the Jewish calendar. Jesus came to represent a Passover lamb on a dripping post, unleavened bread in the oven, and the first fruit of a new harvest season.

The Jews presented their case to Pilate, "This man openly claims to be co-equal with God. Blasphemy warrants a death penalty according to our law. We've already tried him and found him guilty, but under Roman authority we're no longer able to execute him. We need for you to do it." On several occasions Jesus told his apprentices he would be hanged in order to fulfill sacred ancient prophecies, but they didn't fully comprehend, until now. Prophets who lived in different eras over several centuries foretold what would become of Messiah. Jesus may have memorized the scriptures and known what to expect, but there was no way he could have orchestrated the events that transpired.

Had David's kingdom not split; had Judah not been deported; had they not returned with their ancestral records intact and rebuilt the Temple; had Zerubbabel not determined to cede national power to Jeshua, and Jeshua not formed a Sanhedrin; had Babylon not conquered Israel, Assyria not conquered Babylon, the Medes not conquered Assyria and yielded to the Persians so Alexander the Great could lead a Greek invasion and pave the way for a Roman Empire; three hundred and twelve prophetic utterances would not have been manifested in the life of Jesus Christ, many on this holiest of weekends on the Jewish calendar.

Had Jesus not been born in Bethlehem to descendants of two different sons of King David; had his family not fled to Egypt; had they not settled in Nazareth upon their return; had Jesus been arrested or killed by assassins at the direction of the Jewish rulers before this very special weekend; had he been beaten or stoned to death as could easily have happened, the story would have ended differently than prophesied.

Pilate tried to absolve himself by sending Jesus to Herod, the governor of Galilee where Jesus hailed from. Herod was thrilled to finally meet the man he heard so many stories about. "I've been told you're a great magician," he chided to sneers and giggles. Then he continued to taunt, "Show me one of your tricks. Do something for me. Make a fish. Heal somebody."

Herod ordered his attendants to put one of his regal purple robes on Jesus and called him King Jesus to yet more uncomfortable laughter. Instead of rendering a verdict, Herod paraded Jesus back to Pilate, leading the processional. Bitter rivals, Herod and Pilate avoided each other whenever possible. History records they were sharply critical of each other. Herod was jealous of Pilate, and Pilate was annoyed by Herod. They sent negative reports about each other to overseers in Rome. Both were notably ruthless.

Pilate took Jesus into his chamber inside the Antonia Fortress to privately interrogate him. Jesus was stoic. "Will you not speak to me?" urged Pilate. "Do you not realize I hold your life in my hands?"

"My life is in God's hands," Jesus finally acknowledged. "You can do nothing beyond what God allows. Those who disrespect and persecute me are ultimately accountable for my fate. You're a pawn. I don't hold you responsible for what happens to me."

When Pilate asked if he was really some sort of king, Jesus confirmed that he was born to be king. Pilate had to concede Jesus' ancestral credentials. Surprisingly, Jesus disclosed he never intended to become a king in the conventional sense. "I don't reign over a material kingdom," he explained, "I reign with Father in the spiritual domain."

While the interview progressed, priests outside worked the crowd into frenzy. When Pilate offered to acquit Jesus, the crowd repeatedly chanted, "Crucify him". Having determined the priests were jealous, Pilate ordered his soldiers to take charge of the prisoner and give him thirty-nine lashes; Roman terminology for a near-death beating. Forty lashes meant beating someone to death. A similar phrase commonly used later was "beaten within an inch of his life". Blood streamed when brutal guards pressed a crown of thorns on Jesus' head. They put the purple robe back on him, put a cane pole in his hand, and bowed down to ridicule the would-be king. Beaten beyond recognition, and barely able to stand, Pilate again offered Jesus' release.

The chief priests issued a threat. If Pilate didn't condemn Jesus they would send word to Caesar that a radical who sought to rebel against Rome and establish a new kingdom in Pilate's province was allowed to go free. History confirms Caesar had twice before reprimanded Pilate for exercising excessive brute force. Such a report would be seen as defiance toward Caesar and Pilate would almost certainly be demoted.

Jesus was condemned and placed with two other convicted criminals who were slated for crucifixion that morning. By now the news was out and crowds lined the streets. Supporters were subdued as established rulers guided the people to lash out at the imposter who they claimed deceived them. The fickle masses went along.

26

A Hill Called Calvary

Archeologists have discovered several types of crucifixes utilized by Romans in the first century. In at least four known cases timbers were cut into four to six inch square beams of various lengths. The simplest and least efficient crucifix was a single stationary post that extended nine to twelve feet out of the ground. A victim's wrists were tied and stretched over his head to be draped over a peg at the top of the post. Other straps were used to secure his arms, torso, and legs using other pegs. His naked body was subjected to whipping before being left to bleed to death or starve. This mode was used in high traffic public areas, usually for mass crucifixions. Almost all crucifixes were recycled.

The Romans also crossed two eight foot beams to make a narrow "X" to lean against a wall or stationary post. Hands and feet were split and strapped or nailed to the beams, and a makeshift strap was tied to the beams and around the hips and groin to keep the body from slipping down. The weight of the victim's torso and head were unsupported. Sometimes soldiers would spread salt on cuts, or burn their subjects with coals to generate added suffering. People lived for days in this painful and humiliating position.

Where crucifixions were recurring they might start with a pre-planted beam that extended seven to nine feet out of the ground as in the first example. The victim's extended arms were wrapped from armpit to wrist to yet another beam. They lifted the bound naked victim onto the pre-planted beam and notched the crossbeam securely in place. This mode proved cumbersome.

Jesus was most likely hanged on another common cross. A six foot horizontal beam was notched, nailed, and strapped to a twelve to fourteen foot vertical beam. It weighed over sixty pounds. This was the configuration Jesus likely dragged through the hilly streets of Jerusalem about two miles from the Antonia Fortress to Golgotha, derived from gulgalta that meant skull cap in Aramaic. Caves in the hillside made the large stone mound just outside the Damascus Gate in the northwest section of the walled city look eerily like the top of a human skull. The Roman's called the small mount Calvaria. It was also commonly referred to by local residents as Pinnacle Peak. From its Apex one could look over the wall and see much of Jerusalem. Or, those inside could look up and see what was hovering on the hilltop.

Before nine in the morning Jesus marched to his death. Supporters protested while antagonists chanted slurs, spit, and threw rocks at him. Famished, exhausted, dehydrated and having lost a lot of blood from the whipping and the many beatings he endured, Jesus was hard pressed to drag his cross, even under threat of more lashings. Roman soldiers plucked a bystander from the crowd and compelled him to leave his two young sons, Rufus and Alexander, in order to help Jesus carry his burden. Simon, a dark skinned physically robust pilgrim from Cyrene, hoisted the cross over his own shoulder and climbed the steep narrow path along the side of the mountain to the point of execution where a special team of crucifixionists awaited.

They started with Gestus, a Zealot who stabbed a Roman soldier with a dagger. He was cynical and defiant to the end. They quickly and efficiently prepared Dismas who took weapons from a Roman storehouse. They hammered dirty nine inch peg nails into his forearms between the ulna and radius bones near the wrists avoiding major arteries and veins so he wouldn't bleed to death prematurely. They learned nails in the hand could not hold a man's weight when flesh and ligaments tore. Then they bent his knees and nailed his feet so he could periodically hoist himself up to breathe.

The goal of crucifixion was threefold. First, to punish and execute, making criminals truly suffer. Second, Romans sought to humiliate convicts by disrobing them and exposing them to onlookers. They intended to present them as powerless and ashamed. They beat them, whipped them, and taunted them at will. And third, crucifixion was intended to deter others from following a path of crime against the state.

Horizontal beams weren't placed over vertical beams as usually depicted. From nail holes, archeologists now surmise that Romans laid their victims on the vertical beam and drew their arms back to better stabilize and immobilize them. With the spine directly against a rough vertical post, splinters pierced flesh when subjects heaved to breathe. Suffice to say without divulging all the nasty details, this was a horrible way to die, perhaps the worst imaginable. That's precisely why the Roman's employed it.

Those who didn't die of shock survived and succumbed to suffocation when they could no longer extend their legs to fill their lungs. Some lasted for hours. No one lasted a full day on a crucifix of that configuration. The Bible records the world went dark while Jesus was on the cross. Using modern methods and reliable data, astronomers have discovered a one minute and 59 second total solar eclipse over Jerusalem in 29AD and a second one of four minutes and six seconds in 33AD.

His mother, several of the women who supported him, and many of his followers scaled the mountain to be near him at the end of his journey. Only one apprentice, John, is listed among those who were with him at the end. John is the gospel writer who gave us his eyewitness account and recorded what the soldiers and priests said and did.

Christianity was birthed out of Judaism. But even early Christian converts of a non-Jewish persuasion held Jesus' crucifixion as crucial to their faith. Without fully understanding the ramifications of Passover and various prophecies, they were taught that punishment by physical suffering, shedding blood, and a substitutionary sacrifice were integral to spiritual restoration. Like most elements of the Christian faith, adherents don't have to analyze or understand it. They only need to accept and appreciate it.

27

Living Man in a Dead Body

Friday, Yom Shishi, was fleeting. The High Holy Sabbath of Unleavened Bread was approaching sandwiched between the sacred feasts of Passover and First Fruits. The very symbol of national rebellion hung over the commoners' quarters near the market opposite the Temple district across town. Roads west to the Mediterranean coast and north to Samaria, Galilee, and ultimately Europe forked at the base of Mount Calvary. For spite, Pilate put a placard above Jesus' head that read "King of Jews" in Hebrew, Latin, and Greek. No observer could miss it.

Frantically, the priests implored Pilate to take the bodies down before sunset ushered in the special Saturday, Yom Shabbat. Yom Rishon, the first day of the new week would soon follow. Pilate grudgingly obliged them. Neither the Romans nor the Jews could afford to stoke a simmering rebellion. The legal establishment needed to stop quibbling and move on.

Upon orders, soldiers broke the legs of Gestus and Dismas so they couldn't support their weight against the vertical beam of the crucifix.

Though they struggled for breath, both men suffocated in a matter of minutes. They inspected Jesus and found he had already died, and had been dead for some time. To assure his irrecoverable demise they speared him under the ribs. From the lower angle the spear penetrated his heart. The trained professional executioners knew exactly what they were doing.

Blood did not pulse or flow from the wound, but globules slowly oozed out with watery body fluids where they pierced him. In modern times we know the condition as hypovolemic shock. There was no more blood to pump so the heart and kidneys shut down from stress. Jesus' unquenchable thirst was a standard symptom. He was devoid of body fluids and craved liquids like a person with collapsed lungs craves air. His wounds, his ailments, and his suffering were humanly unbearable. He was literally living on empty upon his passing. In a very real sense, "he gave his all."

Gestus and Dismas were likely hurled off the cliff into the burn heap at Gehenna along the southern edge of the city where criminals and unclaimed beggars usually ended up. Oddly, the Sanhedrin used the silver coins returned by Judas Iscariot to purchase burial grounds outside of Jerusalem they called Haqel Dama in Aramaic, or "blood field" in English, for beggars, criminals, and unclaimed bodies. The issue posed a recurring problem for them.

A wealthy merchant unexpectedly intervened to claim Jesus' body and give him a proper Jewish burial in a nearby garden tomb he purchased and prepared for himself and his family. Joseph was the patriarch of a highly regarded family from Aramathea that was known for exquisite silver jewelry. He, like his friend Nicodemus, was a member of the ruling Sanhedrin.

Joseph and Nicodemus had less than two hours to clean and dress Jesus' body and lay him in the grave before sunset of the new Sabbath. Because of their station, it's unlikely they touched the body. They probably directed the soldiers Pilate assigned to help the elderly aristocrats. The soldiers were then dispatched to seal and guard the tomb. One of them may have been the one who gambled for and won Jesus' seamless wool tunic he would soon reappear in. He may have run off and left it so Jesus could paradoxically reclaim what was his. If the seal on the grave door was tampered with or broken the guards would be court marshaled. Darkness set in. It was Sabbath. The nation, and the body, rested.

Inside that tomb a body, and the Holy Bible, assumed life from a different perspective. That which was patently material yielded to its spiritual root. A source, the force behind nature, did not intervene but merely manifested itself. As in the big bang at our inception, upon the behest of an unknowable force, energy took on form and substance in a space time continuum. Creation recreated itself.

A strand of natural maternal DNA withered only to reveal its supernatural synthetic counter-strand. A cell reproduced and began to multiply on a human frame. That which was cut and pierced and punctured became scarred. Scars disappeared according to the directive of each newly manufactured cell in compliance with modern medical knowledge and scientific principles confirmed by stem cell research in recent years.

Initially submissive genes now surfaced to become dominant. Highly efficient DNA rebuilt and revived nerves, muscles and tissues. A body convulsed, lungs filled, a heart beat, a brain awoke. Eyes opened in a dark chamber and a perfect specimen conceived in the image of God stood again on once limp legs. It took only three days for the great physician to totally heal himself.

You don't have to be a religious nut to accept the Bible story. You can be a scientist. You can acknowledge proven accepted laws and principles, test various hypotheses, remain open to expanding truths based on new exposures, and yield to probabilities based on new and known facts. As more light is provided, images become clearer. More knowledge improves perceived probability, but people can only accept what they can believe. Assumed knowledge never trumps absolute faith in any genuine scientific endeavor or pursuit, be it biological, mathematical, or philosophical. That's what drove Archimedes, Newton, da Vinci, Pasteur, Michelangelo, Einstein and Tesla.

When Jesus was born, and at other critical junctures, miracles, apparitions and paranormal activity reached a physical crescendo. Jesus is reported to have been seen and touched by scores of people after his resurrection from the tomb. Thousands of people claimed to see him, sometimes by the hundreds at a time. He supposedly visited his apprentices repeatedly. He spoke, and laughed and even ate.

Josephus, Philo, Eusibius and other historians did not see him personally but alluded to the strange stories that circulated among the common masses. As with the creation of the universe, the advent of life, the appearance of man, or the application of intelligent reason, no one can observe, test, prove or disprove that a figure history identifies as Jesus of Nazareth, a purported Jewish messiah, arose from death. But millions of people through the ages have staked their lives on it.

28

Impact on Observers

In the early hours of Sunday, April 5, 33AD, an earthquake rocked Jerusalem. The Bible alleges there was a prior earthquake on Friday while Jesus was dying on a cross. At that time the Bible states, "boulders tumbled from hillsides and gravestones moved away". The event on Sunday could have been an aftershock. Earthquakes were not uncommon in first century Israel. The area remains geologically active, even today.

Aside from the fact women arrived at the crack of dawn on Sunday morning, nothing more is known or stated about what happened at the gravesite over the thirty-some hour period while Roman guards stood watch. Given the phenomenal number of such novel circumstances recorded in the Bible and in historical accounts, the hours could well have corresponded to Jesus' lifespan in years.

The Bible states that Mary from Magdala, whom Jesus rescued from a life of prostitution, Salome, who could have been either Jesus' half-sister or the mother of his friends James and John, and Mary the mother of James, who may well have been his own mother, came to the tomb hoping to finish cleaning and dressing the body properly. With Jesus supposedly dead, Hebrew custom dictated his mother now be referred to as the mother of her other living children. In this case James, Joseph and Salome fit three of the five siblings mentioned in Luke's gospel. It is interesting that upon the declaration that Jesus had resurrected, she is consistently thereafter called "Mary, mother of Jesus".

Given the circumstances, they may not have known the condition the corpse was left in, or that the tomb was sealed, restricted, and guarded. Ordinarily, they would have been turned away. But when they arrived, the boulder that sealed the entrance was open such that a body could pass. The guards had fled the scene.

Upon Mary the Magdalene's inquiry two figures inside the tomb told her the man she was looking for had come back to life and left through the open door. Eyes filled with tears, and not knowing what to think, she asked a man she presumed to be the steward of the garden if he knew what happened. When he uttered her name she recognized the voice and rushed to clasp his knees.

"Don't cling to me like this," he said. "I'm still transitioning and you cannot hold onto my form. Go tell Peter and the others I am alive and well, and will come to them shortly." The events that follow in the story as presented in the Bible are orderly and rational if one can get past the shock of the initial miracle that prompted them, which for people with healthy faith is not too difficult.

Judas, having panicked when he could not reverse the arrest and conviction he instigated, committed suicide before knowing what would become of his Boss. Like Adam, Cain, and myriads of characters throughout the Bible, he might have fared well had he bowed before God and sought forgiveness and restitution. Instead he is forever vilified in the hearts and minds of people subsequently looking on.

Several of Jesus' men ran to the tomb to find it empty and unguarded. The facial napkin was folded and the linen strips he was swaddled in lay in a heap. If there was a shroud it was not mentioned in scripture. That does not, by itself, necessarily discredit the famous shroud of Turin.

The first day, Jesus made several bodily appearances. Having come for Passover, a young man named Cleopas who had put his trust in the new messiah, walked home from Jerusalem to Emmaus with his wife or an unnamed friend. The two were downcast and dejected when a figure in a hooded tunic like the one Jesus had worn approached as if to pass them. They struck up a conversation and Jesus was able to encourage them by referencing and quoting large portions of messianic scriptures and connecting necessary circumstances and events they would not otherwise have put together.

By the time they recognized who they were listening to, Jesus was gone. They rushed back to Jerusalem and found some of Jesus' apprentices where they were staying in the rented upper room they dined in three days earlier. That evening Jesus appeared to ten of them as they ate. Thomas, who was absent, could not accept their testimony until Jesus personally appeared before him the next week. Such a rejection should come as no surprise to any logic driven reader.

Outside of the gospels there are accounts of Jesus mingling at a gathering of over 500 people, among many other purported appearances. When the apostle Paul addressed the occasion he defied naysayers proposing they talk with eyewitnesses who were still living at the time of his writing around 50AD.

While he lived, Jesus declared he would arise from death in order to conquer the sin that initiated it in Adam's garden paradise. He also said he would not reign in our physical realm, but would take on his ultimate form and provide a counseling spirit that would guide any person who ingested it, or allowed himself to be baptized in it. By design, it was an indwelling spirit, not an external entity.

Jesus dwelled on Earth and navigated the created order, teaching and sharing for forty days before he assumed his ultimate quantum spiritual state and departed like a rising puff of smoke and steam into the atmosphere. No longer composed of raw human genetic material, he left no dust.

Having made post-resurrection visits to his half-brother, James, who in his earthly pilgrimage never fully understood Jesus, and to Saul of Tarsus, a Jewish prodigy bound for the Sanhedrin who became Paul the Apostle upon his confrontation with Jesus along the road to Damascus, Jesus recruited two of the most prolific leaders of his spreading religious contingency.

James became the ring leader over the apostles, and Paul became the chief missionary responsible for establishing the church among gentile, non-Jewish, believers. Both suffered a martyr's death rather than deny what they witnessed, taught, and wrote about. James was taken to the roof of the Temple and told to recant his claims about Jesus. He refused and was hurled to the stone courtyard below where he was met with a barrage of clubs and stones. Paul was imprisoned, tortured and ultimately beheaded in Rome.

In fact, among those closest to Jesus not one broke rank under severe persecution and ridicule. There is ample historical evidence they suffered martyrs' deaths. Matthew was put to the sword in Ethiopia. Mark was dragged by horses through the streets of Alexandria, Egypt. Peter was crucified upside-down on an X styled crucifix because he emphatically proclaimed he was not worthy to die as his master had died. Luke was hanged from an olive tree in Greece by antagonistic idol worshipping priests after converting scores of their followers who never turned back.

James the son of Zebedee and brother of John was beheaded in Jerusalem. So convincing was his testimony at trial that the Roman guard assigned to him knelt with him and demanded to be slain as a Christian alongside him. Nathaniel Bartholomew was whipped to death in Armenia. Thomas was stabbed with a lance in India for establishing churches there. Jude, the younger half-brother of Jesus, was shot with arrows when he would not renounce his faith in Jesus Christ.

Andrew was whipped by seven Roman soldiers and hanged on an X shaped cross like the one described in an earlier chapter. A non-Christian source marveled when Andrew proclaimed he "long desired and expected to die on a cross because it had been consecrated by his master." He lived on that cross for two days and never stopped preaching to and converting those who gathered to ridicule him. Matthias, the apostle chosen to replace Judas Iscariot, was stoned unconscious then beheaded. Barnabas who traveled with Paul was stoned to death in Thessalonica, now Salonika in modern Turkey.

John survived being doused with boiling oil during a wave of persecution in Rome. He was later sentenced to work in mines before spending time in solitary confinement, banished to the rock island of Patmos where he received the visions he penned in his book of the Revelation of Jesus Christ, the last book of the Holy Bible. Upon gaining his freedom, John returned to become Bishop of the church at Ephesus, also called Edessa. He is the only one known to have died peaceably as an old man. He was in his late eighties, scarred, physically impaired, and justifiably revered.

Had the accounts not been so widespread and consistent, or had they been credibly questioned rather than confirmed by early writers, they would have no merit. Considering the unreasonable and violent means by which adversaries of the gospel try to suppress or dispose of those who actively promote it today, the scenario is quite reasonable.

Part 4

The Church Era

29

The Gift of Native Tongues

The original Jewish holiday of Shavuot, still celebrated today, commenced on the eighth Sabbath after the opening Sabbath of First Fruits. The holiday was later recognized as Pentecost in the Greek speaking world, alluding to fifty days. It commemorated Moses' reading of the Law at Mount Sinai fifty days after the Jews were liberated from their bondage in Egypt. By Jesus' time the holiday had grown from a somber reflection after a public reading from the Torah to a jubilant national celebration. Like other religious occasions, the Jews anchored Pentecost to the Temple where the Sanhedrin presided.

What the New Testament Book of Acts refers to as an upper room is usually portrayed as a rooftop or upstairs chamber like where Jesus shared his last supper immediately before his arrest and crucifixion. If 120 people sat to eat, while hundreds looked on in the midst of a crowd of thousands as the Bible describes, that can't be right. Instead, the Temple Mount, where the Muslim Dome of the Rock and Al Aqsa Mosque stand today, suggests a vast courtyard surrounding an elaborate Jewish Temple complex. The courtyard accommodated a crowd of two hundred thousand people who gathered on the Temple grounds early on Saturday morning hoping to get a good seat.

Levites opened storage rooms that lined the interior western wall of the Temple grounds and ran the length of the courtyard. Jews still gather at the now-famous "wailing wall" on the opposite side of that wall forty feet below the Temple elevation. Hundreds of Levite Temple associates, generically called priests or scribes in the Bible, rolled out tables like a modern caterer would prepare an open-air dining hall. Rain and foul weather would have been a rarity in Jerusalem during the month of May.

A roasted lamb was placed on each table with a tray of fruits and a basket of bread. Each lamb served 10-12 people. When Jesus' band of apostles passed dozens of outdoor baptismal mikvahs and ascended the 40 or so stairs to the Huldah Gates entrance on the south side of the Temple grounds, men clamored to greet them. Most of those in attendance were from Judah and Galilee, but many traveled from distant lands to be part of the worship festival.

Jesus of Nazareth was a major topic of conversation, and a major concern for the ruling clerics, at Pentecost the year of his crucifixion. People who had seen or heard Jesus approached his followers as they arrived and might have asked, "We've heard your boss rose from his grave. Is it true? Is he alive now? If he was Messiah, why did he leave? When is he coming back? What should we expect?"

The friends who arrived together surely planned to sit at the same table and eat from the same lamb. But another scenario arises from the Bible. Jesus' disciples spread out to join other parties in order to address their questions, comments and concerns. If eleven men separated and joined full tables they conversed with about 121 men, just as the Bible describes. In the course of the meal each disciple shared his personal testimony and explained that Jesus availed more than a political conquest. Those present listened intently until someone at one of the tables turned to ask his neighbor, "How can you understand this? He's speaking in my native Persian tongue."

"That's strange," his new acquaintance replied. "I'm from Macedonia and I hear him speaking Greek."

"You're both wrong," someone else said. "I'm here from Ethiopia and he's talking directly to me."

Laughter broke out when each one realized that the disciples shared a common Galilean language and dialect, yet everyone who listened to them heard what was said in his most comfortable native tongue. They realized that the "pneuma", which could be translated wind, breath, or spirit, that swept through their midst altered what the apostles said concerning Jesus so it was simultaneously received with clarity and accuracy in a diversity of languages. The term "glossolalia", from which we get the term glossary, denotes structure in languages. Cynical clerics who stood nearby, but weren't privy to the conversations, accused the men in question of being drunk and behaving foolishly. The courtyard erupted.

Simon, whom Jesus nicknamed Peter, stood and commanded everyone's attention. "It's nine o'clock in the morning, for goodness sake," he began. "These men aren't drunk with wine, as you suggest. Today we are experiencing the very event the prophet Joel described." Peter went on to explain that the miracle they were witnessing was to be expected in accordance with what had been prescribed in their sacred holy scrolls over seven hundred years earlier.

Afterward, he proclaimed that Jesus had obeyed the Law, fulfilled the Scriptures, and sacrificed himself to restore spiritual access to physical men. Then Peter invited those present to follow Jesus and repent, or recalibrate, to align with God. Three thousand men determined to accept Jesus as their savior based on the testimony presented and their own personal observations. Upon their baptism most theologians mark this event as the birth of the modern church.

30

The Early Christian Church

The Greek meaning of the word "ekklesia" Jesus used in the Bible did not embrace a building or religious institution. The term we translate as church originally referred to a specific assembly of dignified philosophers and scholars that periodically met in Athens, Greece, before Jesus lived. The movement that advanced the teachings of Jesus as a new faction of Judaism was originally called the "Way". Followers of the Way were predominantly Jews who applied faith and conscience in every facet of life.

The Greek word christos meant anointed one. Christianos would have denoted acquired property of an anointed one. The term Christian as first used at the village of Antioch a little after 40AD was intended as a derogatory slur akin to modern social hate speech. Some adherents of the Way thought others among them shunned personal accountability. A debate arose between those who held that submission and reliance on Jesus as their savior assured their righteous standing before God and those who argued that one had to live out his devotion by adhering to laws and following Jewish rules.

Messianic Jews who first employed the pejorative term Christian believed Jesus Christ's original teachings had been hijacked and corrupted. They objected to people worshiping a man, which clearly violated Jewish protocol, rather than worshiping the God that Jesus humbly and modestly directed them to serve. The "Christian" label came to espouse a thorough transformation by assimilating Christ's Spirit into one's being to live for God as a perpetual act of worship. The original apostles did not object to the new moniker.

Ekklesia katholika ultimately became an open general gathering of likeminded people. Ekklesia Christanos became a gathering for likeminded followers of Jesus Christ. Ekklesia katholika christanos would have been a catholic, or universal, church for Christians. The Way was forced out of existence by legalistic leaders within the Jewish religion and by a hostile Roman government. Christianity evolved into a non-Jewish religious institution.

Today the Christian Church composed of willful men is not a pure reflection of godly righteousness, but its foundation is solid and dependable for those who have faith in the providence of God and the provision of Jesus Christ. The Bible teaches that men are to be "in the world, but not of the world." True Christians have to be strong enough and wise enough to remain spiritually calibrated amid material distractions. When people get off course they need to recalibrate, or repent. That's an individual effort in a corporate environment.

At a campsite near Caesarea Philippi Jesus asked his apprentices what they heard people saying about him when he mingled among them. "Some say you're the greatest teacher that ever lived," one said. Another offered, "They're saying you embody the spirit of Elijah and other great prophets." But Jesus commended Peter when he observed, "You are the Christ, the son of the living God and savior of men." Jesus proposed that Peter was inspired and went on to explain his place in human history as indicated by the sacred scrolls that had been entrusted to the nation of Israel over many centuries.

"Flesh and blood didn't reveal that to you," Jesus proclaimed. "God's Holy Spirit availed your insight." Jesus likely spoke in Hebrew or Aramaic that was later written in Greek. Some contend Jesus suggested the church would arise from Peter (petros) himself, but the text clearly states "upon this rock (petra) I will build my church." Peter is never referred to as petra in scripture. Petros describes a rock that can be lifted and thrown. Petra indicates a cliff or foundation stone. When Jesus alluded to what ended up being rendered as "church" he clearly intended to establish an open assembly of likeminded devotees who would commit to spiritual development above material aspirations so the kingdom of God could be reflected in the habitat of mankind on Earth.

The lesson at the encampment at Caesarea Philippi occurred on a trip Rabbi Jesus took with his twelve talmidim from Galilee through towns and villages in Jordan, Syria, Lebanon, and points north in his second year of ministry. It has been estimated to have covered over two thousand miles and kept the students and their teacher away from home for at least eight months. As they hiked, and when they camped, they talked. The master teacher poured himself into those who would eventually lay the foundation for his church and contend to expand and preserve it through its infancy.

Jesus' half-brother James is known to have become the principal leader of the group of original apostles, those who were actually personally tutored and groomed by Jesus. They attended Temple services on Saturdays, like other devoted Jews, then met on the steps outside the Temple on Sunday mornings to discuss the readings, analyze the scrolls, and augment their understanding of the scriptures from Jesus' perspective as led by the spirit that indwelled them. Together they practiced what Jesus modeled.

The group, moderated by James, consisted of Simon Peter, his brother Andrew, their cousins James and John, Philip, Nathaniel Bartholomew, Thomas Didymus, Lebbius Thaddeus, Matthew and his brother Little James, and Simon who had been a Zealot. Upon Judas' suicide they elected Matthias to replace him. Hundreds met with them and listened in every week. Many onlookers were baptized, or cleansed and imbedded, into what was perceived by establishment Jews as a burgeoning cult.

Several young men followed Jesus' band of talmidim from place to place during the last year or two of his ministry. They were never formally inducted, but grew close to the group. They were the candidates from among whom Matthias was selected to replace Judas. To use a crude analogy, it would be like musicians looking to replace an absent instrumentalist with a proficient artist who personally knew the original band leader and was intimately familiar with his work.

Peter remained a leader among them, but historical accounts, archeology, and scripture indicate that he formally deferred to James who became known as the first Bishop of the Jerusalem Church. As if to validate that Jesus intended to build his "church" on the foundation of Peter's testimony as opposed to a person other than himself, Peter not only deferred to James administratively, but an outsider named Paul became the chief recruiter and architect for what we know as the modern institutional church.

31

Paul, Apostle to the Gentiles

It is impossible to overstate the important influence the Apostle Paul had on the Bible as we know it. He is directly responsible for as many as thirteen of the twenty-seven books of the New Testament and his friend Luke used half the book of Acts to chronicle Paul's life promoting the gospel.

Saul of Tarsus was born in 5 AD at Tarsus, Cilicia in modern-day Turkey to Jewish parents who were Roman citizens. The young genius, clearly a prodigy, was moved from what was then a part of the Roman province of Syria to Jerusalem soon after his bar mitzvah at the age of 12, sometime between 17 and 20 AD. There he began his in-depth study of the Hebrew Scriptures under the famous Rabbi Gamaliel who was credited with being the "scholar of the Sanhedrin".

Saul later identified himself as being a radically dedicated Pharisee of the tribe of Benjamin. He gleaned from the greatest minds of Judaism during the era of Temple restoration. He had access to every scroll and all the legal and historical documents that had been accumulated over the course of the nation's existence. He was privileged, confident, well-educated and absolutely brilliant.

Saul was in Jerusalem the week of Jesus' crucifixion about fifteen years into his grooming for Jewish leadership. When the Sanhedrin met months later to condemn Peter and John and repudiate the Way, it was Gamaliel who proposed that they not take rash action. "If this movement is not of God it will subside and perish like all religious uprisings," he observed. "But if it is truly sanctioned by God, it will flourish and we dare not contend with it."

Gamaliel allied with two known Christian sympathizers in the Sanhedrin; Nicodemus and Joseph of Aramathea. But Saul did not align with his mentor. Whether he was driven by genuine principal, his academic understanding, or political aspiration is unclear. What is known is that Saul sided with the Sadducees and those Pharisees who wished to squelch the movement and preserve the status quo.

Saul was on hand for the stoning of Stephen, a prominent advocate for and teacher of the Way. The Bible records the mob that executed Stephen laid their coats at Saul's feet while they hurled their rocks (petros), indicating he was their ringleader. He seemed unfazed by the fact that Stephen forgave them and prayed for them as he died on the street in a pool of his own blood.

Saul was commissioned to arrest and apprehend other "outlaws" who practiced Christianity within the Jewish religion, charging them with blasphemy. He went door to door in Jerusalem then diligently and deliberately chased those who fled to outlying towns and villages. On his way to Damascus, Syria, to put down the expanding movement and bring its leaders to justice, he confronted a strange apparition.

A radiant light engulfed his entourage in the middle of the road. Everyone in his traveling party fell down and covered their eyes. But when brazen Saul stood to analyze and confront it, a voice spoke to him. "Saul, Saul, why are you persecuting me?" When Saul asked who was speaking, a kindly voice replied, though Saul was the only one who heard it, "I am Jesus. Why do you insist on kicking against the shepherd staff that prods to guide you?" Saul fell to his knees as he was enlightened and redirected.

Saul came to personally believe that Jesus, whom he knew died in Jerusalem, was alive and unleashed in a new different form. He understood the God he sought to study and serve was contained in that same Spirit. At the light's disappearing he was blind and confused. The voice told him to proceed to Damascus where he would meet a man named Ananias who would restore his sight.

Like God changed Abram's name to Abraham and Jesus changed Simon's name to Peter, Saul would henceforth be known throughout the rest of his life as Paul. Recall that God gave Adam and Eve their names and allowed them to give names to what they oversaw. Naming or renaming is a privileged of ownership or oversight. Paul gave himself to Christ with abandon for the rest of his life.

Paul stayed in Damascus to study and debate with those he went there to arrest. He was a changed man, but they knew his reputation and didn't initially trust him. Paul came to understand and accept his adversaries' genuine devotion to Jesus as their long anticipated Christ. It was not what he expected. It wasn't the way he had been taught. He was looking for a worldly political savior whose military conquests would firmly establish Jewish cultural dominance and impose Jewish religious standards in the homeland.

Paul spent a month in Damascus debating the merits of the Way as the culmination of Judaism according to the Law and the Prophets, which he knew by heart. Zealous Jews outside the new denomination within their ranks determined to assassinate him. His advocacy against Christ had been compelling. As he explored and analyzed Jesus' life, teachings and ministry in contrast to the Jewish holy books he saw the light, as it were. He could no longer argue against the manner of worship, salvation and lifestyle that Jesus taught. Paul's appetite for understanding was ravenous, but with his life in peril he could no longer stay in Damascus.

Instead of going back to Jerusalem to confer with the original apostles who still met on the steps of the Temple, or going to other Way gatherings to compare their beliefs and practices, Paul sought seclusion. He spent three years in Arabia studying, analyzing, and reviewing everything he had read and been taught. He prayed for guidance and sought truth and meaning in the scriptures that were the foundation of his life. Guided by the Spirit that now indwelled him, he emerged to become the staunchest advocate and most influential designer of the blossoming Christian movement.

32

The Church's Mission

After three years in seclusion analyzing everything he had been taught, Paul emerged in Antioch, an important Roman city of 200,000 residents where Roman coins of the day were minted in the outlying Syrian province. His reputation for persecuting followers of the Way intact, he was feared and rejected by those with whom he desperately wanted to meet. A local leader of the Way movement by the name of Barnabas befriended Paul at a synagogue and convinced his peers to accept him in their meetings.

Those who heard him were amazed at Paul's doctrinal positions. He parsed ancient scriptures, explained messianic prophesies, and shared what he learned at the feet of Gamaliel and other great rabbis. He uncovered mysteries that had been buried for generations. Like Joseph, Zachariah, and John the Baptist, Paul was born and groomed for his role in the spiritual kingdom that superseded his mortal habitation.

He was an intellectual giant, an academic genius, and a true scientific thinker insofar as he based his reasoning on historical data coupled with firsthand observation, and was open to altering his positions based on new insights and exposures. It would have been very hard to argue with such a man on a quest for truth whose deductions were based on exhaustive research and personal experience.

Paul stated in his writings that, "We wrestle not with physical elements, but with spiritual forces beyond our perception." The Bible dictates, and science confirms, that what we perceive on the surface and accept at face value is not necessarily ultimate reality. There is a force behind nature that cannot be understood or harnessed. Every breakthrough leads to a deeper pursuit.

Paul believed every human is accountable for a unique soul that transcends the physical body in which it resides. He likened his many substantial accomplishments and attainments, and correspondingly his losses and failures, as dung to be discarded relative to the grandeur of understanding Christ and coming into a right relationship with God.

The Antioch fellowship eventually sanctioned Paul, and enlisted him to accompany Barnabas on a trip to the Greek isle of Cypress. From there they passed through towns and villages in what is now Turkey, working their way back to Antioch. They converted multitudes of Jews and Jewish sympathizers everywhere they went. Their mission was to spread "the good news" of salvation through Christ's atoning sacrifice. Succinctly, they taught that the plan unveiled from centuries old Hebrew scrolls was fulfilled in the life, death and resurrection of Jesus Christ.

Paul was formidable in debating Jews and convincing them Jesus was the messiah described in their holy scrolls. But he was especially adept at luring people outside the Jewish faith to accept Jesus Christ as the source and sole object of true spiritual enlightenment. Paul, like Peter, understood that Judaism was the incubator for the one destined to lead all men out of spiritual darkness into restored life.

Paul was an outstanding administrator. Through his example, personal direction, and letters he virtually singlehandedly established the organization and protocol that still guide most churches today.

In Corinth, prostitution was part of a fertility ritual that beckoned a bountiful harvest in Baal worship. Since many Temple priestesses converted to Christianity he advised that women there should not be entrusted to lead men in worship, for obvious reasons. In Galatia worshippers were legalistic, so Paul proposed structure but admonished that good deeds were a reflection of a person's beliefs, not a means of gaining favor with God.

Paul submitted that anyone who aspired to lead should be a person of proven commitment. The litmus test he offered was a man's commitment to his wife in the sanctity of his marriage. James, the Bishop of the Jerusalem church taught that men who were not resolute were like waves on the sea, driven and tossed by prevailing winds. Paul and James modeled commitment and resolve.

The simple message Paul repeated in various venues holds the key to salvation according to the Bible. Everyone eventually sins and becomes detached from the source of life. The result of sin is death, the natural outcome of the unavoidable laws of our existence. God offered the definitive blood sacrifice in the form of a physical man to appease the law no mortal man could adhere to. No one can fulfill what restitution demands, but those who identify with the risen Christ and subject themselves to his divine authority and guidance in their mortal lives are grafted back into spiritual right standing with God.

Jesus invited people to ingest his words and teachings, and make them the sustenance of their worldly existence. Paul professed those who submit to Christ would be saved. They pass from death to a life which knows no bounds and exists beyond present physical form, having been reborn or recalibrated to an eternal spiritual state. Paul declared, "If you confess that Jesus Christ is ultimately in charge, and believe in your heart that God raised him from death, you too will enter the eternal state of Shalom, or absolute peace, contentment, and bliss." The simple premise of Christianity is that a person can avoid death by divesting willful control and assuming a spiritual orientation, submitting to the authority and guidance of a consecrated Holy Spirit.

A lot of people say things they don't really believe. Others conceal what they genuinely believe. Paul scoured the Bible and came up with a simple formula that he carried from town to town and shared with anyone who would listen. Those who have enough faith to accept Jesus, and are willing to say so and live by his precepts, make the transition from death to life. Paul's message, built on Peter's testimony at Caesarea Philippi, is the foundation of the church.

The church's stated mission in the world is not just to gather for worship and learning, but to present that message to those who will accept it and to model it in a genuine and attractive manner. When you hear the terms evangelism and evangelical, that's what they actually mean. Jesus declared that subjects of his kingdom are to be candles to attract and enlighten, and salt to flavor and preserve.

33

End of Earth

In the beginning God created the heavens and the earth. In the end he'll dispose of them. The Bible states everything that's physical will be consumed. Astrophysicists know it's true. In the 1970s scientists calculated that the universe had to start retracting at some point. While some new computer models seem to indicate the universe is expanding at an ever accelerating rate, other recent scientific reports herald that after billions of years the universe is in confirmed measurable decline.

In a Psalm David wrote, "Thy word is a lamp unto my feet, and a light unto my path," referring to the written Torah. The Bible is a route map to expose where we stand and illuminate our way forward. It eerily documents and illuminates the course of mankind on Earth. In the ninth century BC the Bible proposed that every physical element will be consumed as it was introduced, which comports with natural science and the laws of thermodynamics.

God made the physical world. Then he closed the oven, set the timer, and left the recipe to bake. He monitors his concoction and opens the oven at intervals in the fullness of time to turn, baste, or add an ingredient. It will come out just as he planned, right on time. The Bible declares that a thousand years to us is a day to God. It will happen despite our concerns, preferences, or even disbelief.

At a point when humanity grew increasingly self-centered, God salvaged the only righteous people on Earth, washed the planet, and started over, so to speak. It took only a few generations for Noah's offspring to begin to exclude God where it seemed carnally expedient. God plucked a righteous man from a perverse culture to show what happens when someone exalts God. Abraham passed his practices and blessings to his descendants.

When those who were established to be exemplary strayed, God let them taste the fruit of their folly. When they lapsed, God scolded them. When they rebelled, God reprimanded them. When they repented, God restored them. When they got comfortable with their earthly accommodations, outstayed their welcome and got ensnared in an oppressive bondage of their own making, God rescued them. Moses was given clear firm rules and guidelines that did little more than conclusively prove humans cannot possibly measure up to God's standards of morality and virtue.

In the midst of wayward nations God provided a king with a righteous heart who raised his people to prominence. However, King David also strayed and Israel, the so-called people of God, paid for their growing secularism over succeeding generations. At last, God opened the oven to inject his secret ingredient into the pot of human existence. Jesus Christ was the single element that ensured the success of the entire recipe. Two thousand years have passed and the Bible indicates the bell could ring, or the trumpet could blast, at any time.

When that happens, tomorrow or hundreds of years from now, it means the table is set and the feast is ready. Scraps, cuttings and trash from the preparation will be discarded while family and invited guests enjoy enduring pleasure. The Bible likens the occasion to a feast where a proud father enjoys watching his children eat and drink to their heart's contentment.

There are seven major Jewish feasts. Jesus was sacrificed during the Passover holiday. He was buried during the holiday of Unleavened Bread. We got a small taste of renewed life on the holiday of First Fruits. And his Holy Spirit's aroma was unleashed and began to spread at the holiday of Shavuot, or Pentecost. Curious coincidence? Perhaps.

But if it's more than coincidence, if it's programmed like everything else in the Bible, maybe the three remaining Jewish holidays should be analyzed. The Feast of Trumpets calls all laborers from the field when the harvest is declared officially over. It's like a buzzer that ends a contest. Points scored after the buzzer won't count in the tally. Christians look forward to a rapture that will suddenly claim their eternal souls apart from their mortal bodies. Participants on the field will shed their uniforms and equipment.

The Feast of Trumpets leads into the Feast of Ingathering where everyone brings whatever he has produced to be weighed, credited, and remunerated. Everybody gets what he deserves according to what he has earned and contributed; or not. Christians believe each soul will stand before the king of the spiritual domain and bow in awe upon recognizing ultimate reality is not physically based. Christ, the risen king, will mete out punishment based on merit and reward those who depend on his undeserved grace.

The judgments at Ingathering are followed by the holiday celebration of Booths or Tabernacles. Jews move out of their earthly homes and live in tents to remember and reflect on the years men dwelt in the wilderness clustered around a mysterious pillar of fire and smoke under God's provision after they were freed from Egyptian bondage. Christians expect their souls to live on in the presence of God.

Eternal mansions in Heaven are a popular misconception based on Jesus' encouragement to his close friends immediately prior to his execution. "Don't worry," he told them. "You've learned you can depend on God. Now trust me too. I have to leave you physically, but I'm going ahead to prepare a place where we can be together forever. Where my father lives there's plenty of room. If that were not the case, I would have advised you."

In the King James Bible of 1611 the phrase Jesus used that was translated "many mansions" referred to temporary dwellings like military barracks, or perhaps even a luxury resort hotel in our day. It's not the place John described in his revelation. Christians will be gathered and enjoy wonderful accommodation for a thousand years before taking up final occupancy in an eternal abode referred to as "a new heaven and a new earth". In Hebrew the terms hashamayim and haaritz refer to that which is intangible (heavens) and that which is tangible (earth). A new purer form of existence will be created, not altered or re-created. The Bible ends as it begins, with a mystical, but totally logical and scientific premise.

34

Rapture, Tribulation and Judgment

The fact people in the twenty-first century engage in the marvel of complex three dimensional computer animation and work alongside technologically sophisticated intelligent robots while refusing to acknowledge that a source of ultimate intelligence programmed our own reality confirms Jesus' pronouncement, that we "have eyes but fail to see." What the Bible said would happen consistently happened, and that's probably a good indicator of the Bible's credibility regarding the future. As stated at the onset, the Bible is neither a history book nor a science text. It is a testament to the relationship between a sovereign God and people into whom he breathed his spirit.

At their inception even the stars supernaturally aligned to affirm the mystery of mankind's pilgrimage on Earth for a span of roughly 6,000 years from a specific point to a prescribed end in the foreseeable future. Regardless when or how the world began or the shape, size, or mobility of prehistoric life forms; in recognition of every law of chemistry and physics the Biblical narrative points to an eventual climax where, "every knee will bow and confess that Jesus Christ is Lord to the glory of God."

The Bible alludes to a mystery that theologians refer to as eschatology; the study of the end of time. Men explore, interpret, and draw conclusions, but no one can know what's real until truth is finally unveiled. What you choose to believe doesn't change facts or disrupt the natural order, but it does dictate your present reality. The Bible repeatedly states a thousand years is as a day with God, and a day is likened unto a thousand years. God made the world in six distinct days (yom in Hebrew), known to signify spans of time. In the Bible's recorded chronology of man we are nearing the end of six thousand years, or day six. The seventh day, the "Lord's Sabbath Day", reflects a period of rest and worship. However, what we translate as "Day of the Lord" represents a period of judgment, or more accurately, reconciling of accounts.

Man's final millennium, or thousand years, will be ushered in by a person the Bible refers to as Anti-Christ, the antithesis of a savior. He is described as a deceiver, a fraud, and an imposter. The Bible declares that men will be so pre-occupied with wars, famines, disease and pestilence that they will be disoriented, distracted and undiscerning. In a vulnerable state they will turn to one who promises relief and safety. Given today's political climate, it isn't hard to envision folks turning to a powerful, deceptive ruler who holds out the prospect of universal peace and prosperity. The ninth chapter of Daniel, the twentieth chapter of Ezekiel, the twenty-fourth chapter of Matthew, the fourteenth chapter of John, the fourth chapter of First Thessalonians, and the entire book of the Revelation contain prophetic writings dedicated to this mystery. It is sufficient here to render a simple outline of coming events.

Global commerce and international politics will grow evermore complex and create challenges that seem insurmountable. Wars will spread and alliances will form so national armies, regional militias, and local gangs will impose the social order. Drought, famine, and outbreaks of disease will recur on a large scale worldwide. Pollution, geological events, and climate changes will darken the sky and poison food and water sources. Fanatical leaders will radicalize on a large scale. Nuclear style annihilation will appear imminent. Oppressive intrusive tyrannical authorities will suppress the masses in their regimes, and powerless commoners will cower in fear for their lives. So sayeth the ancient Holy Bible.

Specifically, a band of nations will coalesce to attack Israel. A charismatic world leader will intervene and propose a treaty to end hostilities. The treaty will offer a widely secular Israel the assurance of peace by laying down arms. Israel will be assured of worldwide statehood recognition and be given the right to govern themselves and rebuild their Temple over the exposed natural bedrock of Mount Moriah in the courtyard of Jerusalem's present day Muslim Haram al-Sherif. The spot exists and a prefabricated Temple awaits erection upon approval. Despite contrary opinions, the placement most likely would not require the removal of the existing Dome of the Rock. Natural bedrock from Mount Moriah penetrates the courtyard pavement elsewhere. And surprisingly, the original site of the first Temple constructed by Solomon in the tenth century BC and destroyed in 526 BC may actually have been recently rediscovered beneath the ruins of the old Market Square in the present Jewish Quarter in the southern section of Jerusalem. King Herod may have wrongly positioned his second Temple based on errant topography.

That treaty, alluded to thousands of years ago, will mark the beginning of an ominous seven year period of tribulation during which thousands of Jews will converge in the homeland, recommit to their religious heritage, and proselytize their neighbors. Despite ultraconservative Christian interpretation, Jewish ancestral scrolls were destroyed when Jerusalem, its sacred Temple, the altar, and all means of ritualistic sacrifice were sacked in 70AD. Pure tribal ancestry can no longer be confirmed, tribal inbreeding was not maintained by Jewish adherents, and it is not literally required to fulfill eschatological prophesy.

Considering dominant modern Islam to be more of a political ideology than a spiritual agency, during the tribulation period the populace will grow utterly materialistic under a totalitarian governing body that will gain near absolute authority over a fourth of the Earth. Christians will have been raptured and spirituality, where allowed, will be mocked. Yet, thousands of dedicated Messianic Jews will enlighten masses of new converts in an area roughly marked by the Old Persian Empire that included southern Europe, northeastern Africa, much of Russia, and virtually all of what we now call the Middle East.

Three and a half years into this period of tribulation, as Israel reinstates Torah worship in their Temple, the Anti-Christ will break the treaty, assert himself, occupy space in the Temple complex and impose rule over Israel. All commerce, education, and administrative oversight will be monitored by an overarching oppressive alien government.

The Bible describes a virtual beast akin to a giant computer, perhaps a repository of artificial intelligence, coming to life and commanding the allegiance of every living soul. All must pay homage and be branded with chips, or an encrypted tattoo in order to obtain food and merchandise in order to survive. The world will become ruthless and chaotic. Common folks will live in anarchy and suffer physical, mental, and emotional abuse the likes of which men have never dealt with.

Job raised the question, "Why do the righteous suffer?" The answer was that evil exists in a world contaminated by sin where men have severed the cord that binds them to God. In God's absence the world reverts to its original state, without form and void. Where God does not rule, chaos and emptiness reign. The Bible declares men who will not live under the rule of God expose themselves to Satan's domain.

One might ask, "Where is the church? And why is there no Christian influence?" In order to reach the condition described, Bible believers must be removed, or raptured from the face of the Earth. On the front side of the tribulation period institutions and sovereignties that are averse to the Satanic order established in the Middle East will have to be neutralized, disengaged, or eradicated. That includes the United States as a viable world power. We will be absorbed into an impotent secular world governing body or effectively abolished as a significant entity by war, famine, disease, or more likely estrangement from God occasioned by the same socio-political practices that proved to be Israel's repeated downfall. Many theologians argue that we are well along that path.

The Hebrew and Greek terms that render and support a rapture theory more specifically say a living resurrected Jesus will consume his Spirit from the Earth. The word picture portrays a gathering or collection of the Holy Spirit that resides in those into whom it has been imparted, living and dead. That which is spiritual will be removed and that which is physical will remain. Human bodies of Christian people will fall lifeless. In an age of epidemics the secular world will have little regard and pay little attention.

The corporate church is referred to as a body that consists of many members. Similar to the DNA that coursed through Jesus' earthly body, every human cell in the church's body has the capacity to be cloned and mobilized to do his work on Earth as stimulated by signals from a spiritual nerve-center, or cosmic brain. As righteous Enoch vanished from Earth in the midst of his brothers and cousins seven generations removed from Adam, people who constitute the body of the church will suddenly be withdrawn just as, "God took him (Enoch) to himself". The Lord will rapture the church in the same manner he gathered Enoch. Enoch, Noah and Lot are examples of God removing righteous presence to orchestrate judgement on the rebellious nations of a degenerate Earth.

Upon Enoch's departure the Bible declared, "the stench of man's rebellion arose to God's nostrils". One thousand years into patriarchal society Noah was born and lived 600 years before being sealed in an ark for seven days awaiting God's purging of willful rebels. Noah foreshadowed those of Jewish heritage who walked upon the Earth for 6,000 years only to be sealed in the tribulation for seven years awaiting God's judgment that will usher in a day of rest described as a thousand years of peace that ultimately gives way to a final war of wills that culminates in a final judgment which settles the disposition of every soul that ever lived. Only those in whom the Spirit resides will be resurrected to eternal life.

It would take hundreds of pages to adequately argue for and against the circumstances and events attendant to biblical eschatology. Those who are concerned should look into it, those who smugly look forward to it better study it, and those who dismiss it might be in for a brutal shock. Nothing about the matter is pleasant, yet Jesus parted immediately after admonishing his talmidim, "Don't despair. Be of good cheer because I have broken through secular materialism. Next, I'm going to prepare a place for you so that you can be with me forever in my Father's domain. I will return for you. Count on it!"

35

Ultimate Humanity

Science is the pursuit of truth based on exposure and examination. The quest never ends. Pseudo-science is the pursuit of explanations that justify a predisposition or displace ignorance with answers that dispel a nagging insatiable sense of uncertainty. It may or may not lead to actual truth.

The Bible is not a science or history textbook. It's a story book. More significantly, it's an answer book for people with ample faith and sound logic. Jesus said, "The way to truth is a straight and narrow quest, and few people persevere on that path. The vast majority of people are lured to follow after pleasing diversions and comfortable deceptions and miss the way that leads to life."

Each person gets to choose what to believe and the Bible declares, "the just shall live according to their faith." In the end, what a person believed can be easily and objectively measured by what he did. To secularists truth is based in physical reality and men can know and experience ultimate truth and master their reality when they eventually discover the right "tree" and bite into enlightenment. But according to the first chapter of Genesis, spiritual truth existed before physical reality and will only be unveiled at the conclusion of the book of life.

Secularly oriented humans view the world differently than spiritually oriented people. The Bible declares we were created to see our world from God's perspective and do his bidding on the Earth. Jesus proclaimed that he came to, "save us", or "set us free". He admonished us to follow him in death to gain eternal life. What the original language portrays is surrendering a natural preoccupation with material life and recalibrating, or repenting, to an original spiritual template.

When Jesus Christ set out to cleanse the Holy Temple of materialism and corruption, the priests stopped him. They demanded to know why he was intruding on their domain. His simple straightforward reply was that he had come to save them. "From what?" they replied. "Look around you. We're doing fine. We don't need anyone to 'save' us." They were wrong. And so are we.

Man was made "in the image and likeness of God". In that image we are not just physical creatures constituted of randomly evolved elements and charged particles. Each of us is composed of physical, mental, emotional and spiritual facets intricately woven and balanced. In that likeness we are channels of stewardship capable of invoking God's authority and establishing his will to displace chaos with order, darkness with enlightenment, evil with good, and tumult with peace. By imposing our own will we fall from that glorious pinnacle to a lesser state.

We say that we are only human, meaning we have carnal limitations. But if we were truly human as originally designed we would reflect divine order. We need to get back to being human as originally intended because carnality breeds contamination that inevitably ends in corruption and death.

In Hebrew, dying is a perpetual act. Once we contract death, we commence dying and continue to die. Our bodies decompose and revert to the materials we were made of. We may be physically broken down, dispersed, and recycled, yet the atoms, electrons and quarks we were made of continue to exist. E continues to equal MC^2, in rough terms. No one actually knows what happens to individual human spirits, but life itself, "chayei olam", is also perpetual. So then, every one of us needs to be saved!

If you believe ultimate reality resides in the tangible, secular, material, physical elements that surround you, that belief establishes your truth and that determines who, or what, you are. You are a physical being in a material world, period; end of your story, wherever your story ends. On the other hand, if you perceive and pursue a reality beyond what you can see, hear, or touch you have defined yourself as a living soul on a spiritual quest in a material world. The first law of Torah is to acknowledge God exists.

Ultimately, you are either a random transient occupant on a spinning planet in an enormous undefined universe, or you are a designated soul with a mission on Earth. A unique receptor chip in human DNA has existed in every person on God's assembly line. Too few individuals ever respond to the divine signal to activate their receptors. Fortunate few have access to, and read, the owner's manual that Christians refer to as the Holy Bible and come to realize why they even exist.

The Bible illustrates that every person has an innate capacity to inject goodness, kindness, order, beauty, or some measure of God's will into the created order. We also have the capacity to impose dismay, destruction, or despair in pursuit of self-gratification. Each of us either tends God's garden and reaps a harvest or, by willfulness or ignorance, selfishly abuses the harvest and degrades God's garden.

Trying to live a moral life apart from repentance and submission defies every page of the Bible. Every story in the book displays man's tendency to seek physical, mental, or emotional gratification at the expense of a compromised spirit. The basis of Christianity is turning away from the bondage of sin and accepting Jesus as savior in order to reconnect with reality and become God's steward in the paradise he entrusted to each of us. Jesus said, "Seek the truth and the truth will make you free."

To paraphrase First Peter 1:15-17, "Since the one who calls you is holy, be holy yourselves in every regard. Torah says, 'you shall be holy, for I am holy.' In order to please the sovereign Lord, your master and judge, conduct yourselves appropriately while you occupy his garden Earth." The key is not in a man's doing, getting, or achieving, but in each human "being" in the likeness of God. The goal of humanity is simply to think and act as God's ambassador and seriously, devoutly steward the garden he put us in. Living like that leads to "life".

36

New Testament Overview

A contract is a legally binding performance based agreement between parties. A covenant solemnly binds parties in shared aspiration. A testament, or will, dictates the distribution of property rights upon the departure of another.

The Holy Bible can be viewed as a contract amended over time, with one final addendum that modified requirements and simplified terms allowing it to endure. It's a virtual worldwide employment contract in absentia that is consummated upon acceptance and terminates upon departure.

An unseen spiritual force we recognize as God, by means beyond mortal comprehension, offers rewards in exchange for devoted allegiance as measured by intellectual assent and physical behavior. In simple terms, God offers to hire workers He "fathered" in a world He created, who are willing to set aside personal interest and self-gratification and tend to a prescribed portion of His garden paradise over a period of time in compliance with His demands according to His sole intentions, and He commits to compensate them with full adoption for meeting their obligation.

It is a unilateral contract in that one party establishes the terms and another, by acceptance in the form of adherence, obligates himself to their fulfilment. It is an open contract in that the offering party allows individuals to participate or reject His offer by their own discretionary acquiescence and conformance. It is a benevolent contract in that the accepting party who has no voice in the matter of terms and compensation stands to benefit greatly from the offering party's estate. And it is a perpetual binding contract in that once it is initialized it cannot be retracted.

The original covenant prescribed that a human being should be entrusted to oversee the affairs of Earth to ensure and spread God's righteous dominion. When the first true man satiated his personal will and sought physical gratification over spiritual union, he sinned and violated his part of the agreement. He broke the law. The contract would have been voided if the Adamic amendment did not restore order. Men would henceforth contend with worldly forces to impose God's domination over a material kingdom. Adam, though expelled from paradise as it was initially established, communed with God and struggled against the elements of his physical nature.

The Jewish Torah establishes that the life of every creature is contained in its blood. Death availed a new covenant, but men did not adhere to that covenant either, and those disposed toward noncompliance were eradicated. A Noahic amendment allowed for repopulation and dissemination of godly dominion. Clans and cultures diverged and became more secular over time until that covenant too became unrecognizably diluted and perverted.

God tapped a man on whom He heaped yet another amendment whereby a human entity would stand out as exemplary to bless and influence those outside the realm of acceptability. Abraham, though imperfect, was found suitable on the basis of his feeble righteous disposition toward God.

Abraham's descendants grew evermore carnally oriented. They grew so comfortable and dependent on sustenance provided in a foreign context they fell into secular bondage. The Mosaic amendment liberated them and set up a strict code of divine law that imposed a routine preoccupation with God's engagement with men on Earth. The Mosaic covenant served to prove over time that men who exert their will on Earth also readily impose their will in the exercise of institutional religion. Though they adhered to the letter of the law, they abandoned the spirit of the law.

When men failed to conform and comply, God availed the Davidic covenant whereby a leader would arise to conquer oppressive adversaries and govern those in his earthly jurisdiction by divine standards. But David also fell prey to evil influences and the nation was lost again.

From the opening pages of the Bible the drama of every man's pilgrimage on Earth was set. Those who were custodians of the original contract of old covenants under the first testament looked for an ultimate Messianic covenant. Caught up in a secular arena, they anticipated material blessings and worldly domination. That was not God's intent. The God of the Bible never obligated himself by contract to be man's servant in this world.

At a predetermined point in time a hominid form like Adam, whom we know as Jesus Christ, was infused with the essence of God. Divinity fully merged with humanity when the living Spirit of Holiness was embedded in a physical human for only a second time. A new will and testament replaced the original contract without displacing it. The law was not nullified or disposed of, but fulfilled. A new and lasting covenant, espousing all the former ones, waits only for its ultimate final disposition while it continues to be executed.

We view the Old Testament as the history of the Jewish people and the New Testament as the tale of Jesus' life and establishment of the Christian church.

Hogwash! In its totality the Bible is one incredible story. All the Bible stories heretofore addressed constitute a complex contract between the God of creation and all people He invites to help steward His created order.

We do not engage on our terms. We die to self, leaving a physical shell to be occupied by a spiritual source. While we live, we actively purge our material inclinations in favor of spiritual inspiration and guidance. We repent to reorient ourselves to the original divine source of our humanity. In a nut shell, we surrender to the sovereignty of God through the lordship of Jesus Christ to be endowed with His Holy Spirit that will convict, console, comfort, and direct any person who will avail himself and respond to His unctions. We are supernaturally baptized, or spiritually born, into His domain. We see the world differently so we act differently.

The New Testament discloses the life, nature, and redeeming authority of Christ. The entire Bible is a course in salvation from death to life in a spiritual sense. Read it again, now that you know what you're looking for. "Hear this, Yisra El. The Lord your God is the sole source of everything. Love, cherish and honor God with all your heart, with your entire mind, and with every fiber of your strength. Jealously protect your spiritual health and commit to ensure the God-honoring best interests of others. You are a steward in God's garden." Turn your receptor on, tune in, and do as the one and only true and living God directs you to do. Jesus died so we could live. In turn, we die so He can live again in us. End of Story. Take up your cross, and follow Him. I hope to see you in Paradise… Amen!

www.ingramcontent.com/pod-product-compliance
Lightning Source LLC
Chambersburg PA
CBHW032119090426
42743CB00007B/398